Will There Be Peace
in
Myanmar?

HS PRESS

Will There Be Peace
in
Myanmar?

**Spiritual Interviews with the Guardian
Spirits of Aung San Suu Kyi
and Gen. Min Aung Hlaing
and Messages from Shakyamuni Buddha**

Ryuho Okawa

HS PRESS

Contents

CHAPTER ONE

My Sorrow for Myanmar and Plea for Help
Spiritual Interview with the
Guardian Spirit of Aung San Suu Kyi

CHAPTER TWO

The Truth about the Coup and China's True Aim
Spiritual Interview with
the Guardian Spirit of General Min Aung Hlaing

CHAPTER THREE

Summing up the Myanmar Problem
Spiritual Messages from Shakyamuni Buddha

EXTRA CHAPTER

Messages from Space Regarding the Coup in Myanmar
UFO Reading 61 (Wilmar from Planet Wilmar)

3 The Wilmarian's Sorrow and Plea for Help

Afterword

Preface

A Buddhist country is in turmoil. A military dictatorship is taking control of Myanmar, a country which believes in a religion that wishes for peace the most.

Some people believe that Karl Marx, who condoned violence, and his philosophy will save the world. Others attempt to conquer the world by advocating "Political power grows out of the barrel of a gun," a phrase coined by Mao Zedong.

Myanmar (Burma) is a tragedy. Will it be the second Tibet? Or will it be brought under a rule of terror like Hong Kong?

I must not be the only one shedding tears seeing soldiers shoot citizens and monks with live ammunition.

Firstly, there comes judgment on whether something is good or bad. Secondly, there come appropriate opinions on it and the international efforts to contain it. Lastly, there comes action with courage.

We should not abandon Daw Aung San Suu Kyi. The Japanese government should take action and seek for her release.

Ryuho Okawa
Master & CEO of Happy Science Group
Mar. 19, 2021

CHAPTER ONE

My Sorrow for Myanmar and Plea for Help

Spiritual Interview with the Guardian Spirit of Aung San Suu Kyi

*Originally recorded in Japanese on March 11, 2021
at the Special Lecture Hall of Happy Science in Japan
and later translated into English.*

In this chapter, there are a total of three interviewers from Happy Science, symbolized as A, B, and C, in the order that they first appear.

Aung San Suu Kyi (1945 – Present)

Politician and pro-democratic leader of Myanmar (Burma), and the daughter of the country's independence hero Gen. Aung San. After she came back from studying in Britain in 1988, she founded the National League for Democracy (NLD) and served as its chairperson, but was detained and put under house arrest by the military government, intermittently until 2010. In 1991, she was awarded the Nobel Peace Prize. In 2012, she became the chairperson of NLD and won a seat for Parliament. In November 2015, NLD won a landslide victory in general election against the military government. In the 2020 general election, NLD once again won an overwhelming victory, but Suu Kyi was once again detained in the coup carried out by the *Tatmadaw*, Myanmar's army, on February 1, 2021.

1

The Myanmar Issue Is of Little Concern in Japan

Myanmar has moved back and forth between military dictatorship and democracy

RYUHO OKAWA

Good morning. Today's theme is the issue of Myanmar or Burma. The title is, "Will There Be Peace in Myanmar?" I do not think Japanese people have sufficient information on this matter. Perhaps they only have a vague sense that something is going on in Myanmar. I think they have little concern about the country.

We would like to hear opinions from the guardian spirit of Ms. Aung San Suu Kyi and find out what kind of person the army general who led the coup is. I am not sure if we can talk with him. I have not made contact with him yet, so I have no idea what kind of person he is and if we can talk with him, but I will give it a try.

As for Ms. Suu Kyi, based on my brief encounter with her guardian spirit, she seems to be quite weak. She is already 75 years old, so she may die from prostration if she continues to be detained under house arrest. So, I am not sure if we can have a lively conversation with her.

Japanese people do not know much about Myanmar. They know much less about Myanmar than about Hong Kong or Taiwan. Japanese newspaper and television sometimes report on Myanmar, but I do not think people can easily understand Myanmar's history of several decades. There have been several military coups in the past, and the country has moved back and forth between military dictatorship and democracy.

Ms. Suu Kyi has a tragic history

RYUHO OKAWA

Ms. Suu Kyi is the daughter of Myanmar's Father of the Nation General Aung San, who was assassinated when she was two years old. Then, she got married to a British researcher on Tibetan culture, and this led to the amendment of the Burmese constitution, which is now preventing her from becoming president.

She studied at Oxford University, and from 1985 to 1986, she lived in Japan as a visiting researcher at Kyoto University's Center for Southeast Asian Studies. I remember this, too.

She formed a political party and is leading it, but things are not going well. She has often been placed under house arrest. Judging from her background, she has a tragic history. She received the Nobel Peace Prize during house arrest, but the military can get even more furious when she does something like this.

How Myanmar's military carried out the coup

RYUHO OKAWA

She is a Nobel Peace laureate and has won in the recent election, but as you may have heard, there is the Rohingya issue, which is complicated.

When the military carried out clearing operations against Rohingya, a Muslim minority group in Myanmar, they fled to Bangladesh as refugees. Now, they are working to come back. Regarding this issue, Ms. Suu Kyi tried to appease the military. As a Buddhist-majority country, it is difficult for Burma to coexist with Muslims. She did not condemn the military's violence against Rohingya, so she came under fire internationally for failing to speak out against the atrocities in spite of receiving the Nobel Peace Prize. She was at a loss, and that is when the coup occurred this February.

In the November 2020 general election, the NLD led by Ms. Suu Kyi won a landslide victory. NLD stands for "The National League for Democracy," but the Japanese people have little idea what it does. Although the NLD won a landslide victory, there was a coup in early February.

I am afraid newspapers do not help you understand... [*Holds up the manuscript.*] This is the manuscript of *Kuro-Obi Eigo*[1]. Now, *Kuro-Obi Eigo 11 Dan Vol. 4* has been published, and we are now making halfway through *Kuro-Obi Eigo 12 Dan Vol. 4*. I am not sure how it will look when it gets published, but I included in the first part some articles covering Myanmar's coup in detail.

According to them, the Myanmar military came to arrest people before roosters crowed the break of dawn. It is after all Myanmar, or Burma. The articles say that the coup was carried out before dawn, before roosters crowed and monks went about asking for alms with bare feet. This is very clear and easy to imagine what happened there.

Protests by citizens and monks against the military, and military crackdown

RYUHO OKAWA

It is quite difficult to protest against the military. In 2007, the documentary film of Burmese protests that was recorded on hand-held cameras became known to the world after being nominated for an Academy Award for Best Documentary Feature. The footage about what was going on in Burma was smuggled to Oslo and broadcast around the world by CNN and BBC. There is such a documentary film that reveals how things really were in Burma.

The citizens relied on monks, and about 400,000 Buddhist monks marched with bare feet holding their alms bowl upside down. They joined hands with the citizens and confronted the military, trying to overturn the military government. But they suffered terrible oppression and many monks were killed. They are also under pretty difficult situation now.

The demonstration on main streets could be subjected to a concerted attack by the military. It's dangerous for people to hold mass demonstrations because the military could open fire on them, so they are protesting on back streets. The protesters pasted copies of photos of Senior General Min Aung Hlaing on the streets and protested by marching on them.

When the military and police try to enter the back alley by car, they find lots of photos on the streets. They think that if they trample on them, they will receive punishment, so they have to pick them all up before they chase the demonstrators, but while the military does so, the protesters flee. So, it is becoming like a cat-and-mouse game.

The Western countries do not recognize Myanmar's military government whereas Japan recognizes and negotiates with it

RYUHO OKAWA

In yesterday's newspaper (Mar. 10, 2021), the Japanese government offered to aid over two billion yen regarding the Rohingya issue. It mentioned another aid, but it treats the military regime as the official government.

The fact that other countries such as the U.K. and the U.S. use the name "Burma" instead of "Myanmar" means they will not recognize a military government. Japan immediately recognized the military regime and calls it Myanmar, so I have no choice. Unlike Japan, the U.K. and the U.S. refuse to change the way they interact with the country. The current situation seems to remain uncertain and I feel Ms. Suu Kyi is in the depths of despair.

Summoning the guardian spirit of Ms. Aung San Suu Kyi to ask her for her opinion

RYUHO OKAWA

I would like to investigate these issues. If they cannot help us much, we should ask Shakyamuni for his opinion, since Burma is a Buddhist country even today.

In what language should we speak? Ms. Suu Kyi can speak in English, but in Japanese... Well, since she was studying at Kyoto University for some while, I think she can speak Japanese. However, I do not know much about Mr. Hlaing. He studied law at the Rangoon Arts and Science University (now Yangon University) and then was admitted to the Defence Services Academy, so he may be able to speak English, but I am not sure if his guardian spirit can translate Burmese into Japanese. So, I think you [*points at the interviewers*] are conscious about this issue, and the map on the wall of Master's Holy Temple shows there are about eight Happy Science believers in Myanmar. Maybe there are more.

A

Yes. In addition, there are 84 believers of Burmese nationality in Japan.

RYUHO OKAWA

There are some within Japan.

A

Thirty-four of them are devotees. (At Happy Science, "devotees" refer to members who have pledged their devotion to the three treasures—Buddha, Dharma, and Sangha.)

RYUHO OKAWA

There are 34 devotees. Then, it is possible to contact or have a relationship with Myanmar. I am counting on them, but I think Japan will be slow in taking action. The Myanmar issue is a much lower priority for Japan. The Japanese media only cover issues such as COVID-19, internal affairs, and anti-government news, so Japanese people have little interest in the Myanmar issue.

Ms. Suu Kyi can probably communicate with us, so I will summon her first.

[*Puts hands together in prayer.*] Then, I will summon the guardian spirit of Ms. Aung San Suu Kyi, the leader of NLD and state counsellor of Myanmar. The guardian spirit of Ms. Aung San Suu Kyi, the guardian spirit of Ms. Aung San Suu Kyi, please come to Happy Science Japan. We would be grateful if we could hear your opinions about the situation that you are in now, your thoughts, your hope, and your expectations for Japan. The guardian spirit of Ms. Suu Kyi, the guardian spirit of Ms. Suu Kyi.

[*About 10 seconds of silence.*]

2

China's Aim behind Myanmar's Military Coup

The guardian spirit of Ms. Suu Kyi grieves over her powerlessness and seeks for help from Buddha

AUNG SAN SUU KYI'S GUARDIAN SPIRIT
Umm, hmm...

B
Hello.

AUNG SAN SUU KYI'S G.S.
Umm, ah, ah, hmm, hmm. Hello.

B
Are you the guardian spirit of Ms. Aung San Suu Kyi?

AUNG SAN SUU KYI'S G.S.
Yes, I am.

B

Thank you for coming here today.

AUNG SAN SUU KYI'S G.S.

My pleasure.

B

Now, you are in a very difficult situation.

AUNG SAN SUU KYI'S G.S.

[*Sighs.*]

B

The coup occurred in February, and the international community is paying attention to what is going on in Myanmar. So, I think this is a very precious opportunity to directly receive your messages.

AUNG SAN SUU KYI'S G.S.

Exactly. I can no longer get outside. I cannot get interviewed. I am really in trouble. From a broader perspective, the world's theme seems to be "the battle between democracy and military dictatorship."

In fact, it is tough for ordinary citizens and barefoot monks alone to fight the military. There is nothing more we can do on our own without foreign media coverage, economic sanction, or military intimidation.

I am not sure how many times I have been arrested, detained, and placed under house arrest by the military. May Buddha save my country! What am I supposed to do? We have no future.

B

I understand you are in a terrible situation. Since Myanmar is a Buddhist country, you are seeking for Buddha to save it, right?

AUNG SAN SUU KYI'S G.S.

There is nothing we can do once the military starts killing monks. We cannot fight unarmed.

Another problem is Muslim immigrants. I think we need to promote some reconciliation policy toward them, but Islam is a religion that allows people to fight. So, as you see it in Burma or Thailand, once Muslims enter the country, Buddhists and even monks start arming themselves with weapons. Otherwise, they would be defeated by Muslims.

Both Muslims and the military have weapons. It is quite difficult to live together in peace with them.

What Xi Jinping intended to do by visiting Myanmar and meeting with the military leader amidst the coronavirus pandemic

B

In addition to the domestic problem of Rohingya, the international situation surrounding Myanmar is becoming quite difficult. For example, Mr. Xi Jinping has a keen interest in Myanmar because it could become a part of the One Belt One Road Initiative. Also, the U.S. is about to change its diplomatic policies after the Biden administration took office. I believe now is the time when you want to send some message to the international community.

AUNG SAN SUU KYI'S G.S.

Yes. I am sending out messages to Mr. Biden asking him not to forget Burma, but I am not sure to what extent he will take action. In January 2020, when the coronavirus was becoming a problem, Xi Jinping visited Myanmar and met with our military leader. They ironed out differences of opinions and shared common interests.

The Myanmar military approved of China's ambition to change everything to their "one country, one system" and bringing Hong Kong and Taiwan under Chinese control. In return, China recognized and supported Myanmar's military government.

The junta knows that the country will face sanction from the West, so it wants to make sure that China will support it even if it is criticized by the international community. Then, when our political party swept the election, the military launched a coup. It is almost like a fixed race. The military intended to carry out a coup from the beginning.

Xi Jinping visited Myanmar last January, when the novel coronavirus started to spread around the world. His move shows he is a good strategic thinker. His intent to take control of Asia by taking advantage of the worldwide chaos is obvious. The military government will be able to take hold of the country if it receives military and economic support from China, so economic sanctions won't work.

B

So, you think China has been involved in the military coup this time?

AUNG SAN SUU KYI'S G.S.

Actually, China is probably trying to establish a puppet regime. Now is the age of international politics, but Burma has been in turmoil between military rule and democracy ever since it gained independence from Britain. Hong Kong also gained independence from Britain, but Hong Kong people now say they prefer the older days when they were under British rule.

I don't know if Asia is behind the times. Hmm, I want to do something about it. I wonder why Japan failed in its revolution to democratize Asia. I have some questions about that.

"I want to make Burma a country of parliamentary democracy, wealth, and high morals"

B

Although Myanmar had been under military rule for a long period of time, Ms. Suu Kyi has been recognized by the western world as a pro-democracy leader and she has won the Nobel Peace Prize.

Do you have an ideal image or vision of Myanmar you want to realize?

AUNG SAN SUU KYI'S G.S.

As a person who experienced Western society, I wanted to realize parliamentary democracy. Japan, too, is much wealthier and has high morals. I wish Myanmar could be such a country.

Japanese people may think that the Japan Self-Defense Forces (JSDF) do not work and are useless, but it will really help if Myanmar's military can discipline itself like the JSDF. If the military acts recklessly, it gets out of control. The troops actually shoot citizens. They raise one knee, raise a rifle, and shoot. I cannot bear to watch.

The Myanmar military regime thinks it is using China, but in fact...

C

You mentioned earlier the relationship between China and the junta. In relation to this, I would like to ask more questions, so that the international community gets a better understanding of it.

Seeing what happened over the past 10 years, I feel that many people around the world are paying attention to what the military really thinks. During the last 10 years, China has strengthened its intervention in Myanmar, and seeing this, the military regime could not stand it and began to welcome the U.S. under the Obama administration. At that time, the military made some concessions regarding the Suu Kyi-led democratization movement.

The military has some connection with China, but as you said, it was afraid of having Myanmar be taken over by China. So, it seemed to be double-dealing. However, now the situation has turned around, which really surprised me.

How do you think the military really feels about China, and what do you think about the military's two-faced nature?

AUNG SAN SUU KYI'S G.S.

I think that the military is just trying to use China. On the other hand, during the Vietnam War, China supported the Viet Cong that fought against the U.S., and the war eventually turned into the war between Chinese and U.S. forces. As the U.S. was defeated, the whole Vietnam became a communist country. I think China is thinking of a similar scenario. China should be anticipating a possible intervention by the West.

Myanmar's military is trying to use China just to receive support, but China is attempting to take over our country. So, they are in the palm of China's hand. If the junta really depends on China for support, our country will be taken over. Mainland China itself does not want democracy.

If China recognized pro-democracy forces like us, then Hong Kong and Taiwan would be able to survive. China is aiming at establishing a totalitarian regime in one stroke, and thinking about attacking Hong Kong and Taiwan from both sides to put them under control.

We are being targeted because China sees us as being weak.

C

Do you mean the military has almost sold their soul to China?

AUNG SAN SUU KYI'S G.S.

They pretend to show respect to Buddhism and make superficial negotiations. They are trying to manipulate people's minds, but deep down, they just want to seize power.

What is in the mind of Mr. Xi Jinping, who is intervening in Myanmar?

B

One of the reasons for China's intervention in Myanmar is geopolitical interests. China can get easy access to the Indian Ocean from Yunnan Province, the inner part of China, through Burma.

Under these circumstances, the military staged a coup, which could mean China intervened. What are your thoughts on this?

AUNG SAN SUU KYI'S G.S.

What Xi Jinping has in mind is as simple as this: China used to rule the Indochinese Peninsula. It's something like that. He wants to take over the entire region and wants hegemony over the South China Sea.

He intends to prevent anti-Chinese countries from passing through the waters of Asia. This is his aim. Oil from the Middle East can only pass through waters under Chinese hegemony, and steel and coal from Australia will need to pass through China-controlled seas, which will push the U.S. back eastward.

In fact, Xi Jinping probably thinks nothing of the U.K. because he is already aiming to take over Europe. However, European countries such as the U.K. and Germany have started anti-Beijing movement over the issues of Hong Kong and the Uyghur region. So, we cannot allow ourselves to easily succumb to China.

3

Hopes and Disappointments regarding Japan and the West

Japan is allergic to military affairs, but not willing to express opinions to other countries

B

Then, the political turmoil is not an issue confined to Myanmar alone, but a theme of international affairs. So, do you have any message to deliver to the Western society? Also, you have an experience of living in Japan and know well about the country, and some Japanese people know you very well. Do you have any message to the Japanese people?

AUNG SAN SUU KYI'S G.S.

The Japanese people gave me a lot of support. When it comes to democracy vs. military dictatorship, Japanese people are allergic to military affairs concerning their own country, but I feel they are not so willing to express their opinions to other countries.

Japan is thinking about the factories that shifted over from China. The Chinese labor costs have soared, making low-cost production difficult unlike it used to be. Japanese companies are now trying to make countries like Thailand and Myanmar the "world's factory," and China's goal is to stop this. They intend to threaten Japan into thinking, "It is dangerous to shift manufacturing to a country of such political instability. We cannot secure the safety of Japanese nationals." Their only objective is to cause chaos.

C

Then, we should call on or persuade the Japanese government to become aware of China's real intention.

AUNG SAN SUU KYI'S G.S.

Even if you persuade the government, it only thinks of giving money... giving money to Rohingya. I am not sure whether doing that will turn out positive or negative. What is more, the Biden administration could support Rohingya and intensify Myanmar's internal conflict.

C

The Japanese government has a rather optimistic idea that things would work out if it keeps the channels of dialogue open to the military dictatorship and make some adjustments. Could you give us your views on this?

AUNG SAN SUU KYI'S G.S.

The U.K. and the U.S. do not recognize "Myanmar" and keep using the name "Burma," whereas Japan was one of the first to recognize the junta. Also, after the Tiananmen incident, which China continued to deny, Japan quickly admitted China's denial and sent the emperor to China, made China rich through trade, and brought ruin upon itself. Japan disappointed us regarding this.

C

So, that is why I think we should send a clearer message.

AUNG SAN SUU KYI'S G.S.

It is true that people like us or Asian and African countries who experienced colonial rule have anti-Western sentiment. The Western countries actually have highly advanced civilization, so we have to come close to them as much as possible. If we cannot get close to them, those in authority will take complete control of the country. Absolute monarchy or emperor would suppress the people, or a military dictatorship would rule the country. This is the reality of the second-tier nations or below.

The Vietnam War was a trauma for the U.S., so they will only go as far as economic sanctions

C
Is there anything you expect of the U.S. or the U.K., who used to be Myanmar's colonial ruler?

AUNG SAN SUU KYI'S G.S.
Things are pretty tough. I am sure that the Vietnam War was a terrible trauma for the U.S. The war was prolonged, and more than 50,000 Americans were killed. More than a million locals were killed, and as a result, a communist regime was established in Vietnam. But now, they restored the relationship with the U.S. because they have anti-Chinese sentiment despite being a communist country.

Then, what was the war all about? Young, great minds of America at that time came up with a logic, but what was it for? It raises doubts.

I do not think the U.S., who still remembers the quagmire of the Vietnam War, wants to be drawn into the morass of war in Myanmar, which they know little about. The U.S. might impose economic sanctions, but they might not go beyond that.

Ms. Suu Kyi's view on the coup occurring soon after President Biden took office

B

Chronologically, in Myanmar, there was the presidential election in November 2020 and the Diet session in February 2021. At the same time, the new Biden administration was inaugurated in the U.S. and the coup occurred when they were shifting over from Mr. Trump's policies.

Some people speculate that China is seeing how the Biden administration will move. What's your take on this?

AUNG SAN SUU KYI'S G.S.

I am afraid that the demonstration in support of Mr. Trump is considered the same as Myanmar's coup. In his speech, Mr. Trump called on his supporters to walk down to the Capitol, and mainly Republicans including some Democrat provocateurs stormed the Capitol and occupied it. This was considered in parallel with the military coup in our country.

I do not know why an incumbent president needs to stage a coup, but people accused Mr. Trump of conspiring it. I feel that Americans are confused about their own values. So, the issue of democracy and military strength is difficult.

In the case of the U.S., people might have had guns whey they stormed the Capitol. But then, 10,000 or 20,000 National Guard troops were deployed when President Biden took office. They protected the Capitol and the White House. It was an unusual inauguration.

The coup on February 1 in Myanmar occurred just after Biden became president on January 20, so we should think that they are connected. China is pulling the strings behind the scenes regarding these matters.

B

It makes perfect sense because the Chinese Minister of Foreign Affairs Wang Yi visited Myanmar in January and met with Senior General Min Aung Hlaing, who led the coup.

AUNG SAN SUU KYI'S G.S.

China is thinking quite strategically. So, a country without sound strategy will fall.

A

Thank you.

4

Japan's Mission as an Asian Superpower

Anticipating how the U.S., U.K., and UN will deal with the Myanmar issue

A

Now, we are talking about the issue of democracy vs. military dictatorship. This morning, BBC reported interviews of police officers from Myanmar. They said the military told them to fire at the citizens and that the military would take responsibility. But they said they couldn't shoot citizens and fled across the river to India, and are going to stay there for a while.

The protests are going on all over Myanmar, so the country might not be functioning properly. The world is watching whether the military will be able to control the people, or how much the public backlash will affect the politics. And you...

AUNG SAN SUU KYI'S G.S.

Yes, some public servants and police officers are participating in the strike... protests. And, what's your question?

A

The military wants to oppress the people who won't obey them. How much pressure do you think they will need to apply to the people to control them?

AUNG SAN SUU KYI'S G.S.

Basically, this is what the UN has to think about. But because China is a permanent member of the UN Security Council, they cannot organize the UN forces. So, there will have to be the coalition of the willing, but I am not sure if it will be formed.

China should be intervening in Myanmar thinking that Biden cannot make decisions. China thinks Biden cannot do much for Myanmar. Helping Myanmar has little benefit for America. Also, can the U.K. help Burma on their own? Burma gained independence from the U.K., after all. Does Johnson, who almost died, have the strength to help both Burma and Hong Kong? Hmm... I don't think he will be able to make any decisive moves.

She is concerned about the Myanmar problem spreading to other Southeast Asian nations by the domino effect

C

In summary, you are saying we need to form an international opinion against China's ambition. And, you expect countries to take further initiative to remove obstacles, in other words, you want to get the countries of concern involved and show your intention to China.

AUNG SAN SUU KYI'S G.S.
Yes. For now, we are almost like "a deer in the headlights." There is nowhere to run. It is as if a snake is waiting for the opportunity to attack its prey. But our country won't be the last.

In Thailand too, the military is denying democracy and should be forming a conspiracy against the king. Also, China is going to take over the regions where the ethnic Chinese are active, so Singaporeans should be aware that they could lose their country. Such a small country can never defend itself.

China is attempting to bar the U.S. and European countries from Asian waters. Japan used to be much stronger, so I am hoping Japan will do something for us.

C

Yes. In short, we should launch a campaign to make the world realize that this is not a problem only concerning Myanmar.

AUNG SAN SUU KYI'S G.S.

No, it is not. It's not. Countries will fall one after another by the domino effect.

China thinks nothing of Myanmar. They are now thinking as far as to seize control of India. They are thinking of crushing India before it grows enough to dominate Asia.

"I would be grateful if Japan would think about realizing proactive peace in Asia"

C

Then, this will be an issue of the entire Asia, so Asia should take the initiative, namely Japan. That is what Japan should do.

AUNG SAN SUU KYI'S G.S.

Yes. I would like Japan and India to join hands as Buddhist countries to come to help us. The Japanese government is concerned about the safety of the Japanese company workers in Myanmar and probably thinking only about having them return home. But Japan should cooperate with India, economically and militarily, and protect peace in Asia. Get the Philippines involved, too. If the situation stays as it is, China will have complete control over Asia, so we have to think about driving a stake into China.

The Western countries have the trauma of having colonized us in the past. They cannot actively help us. They cannot unless we ask them.

C

Then, there are lots of things Japan can do, such as enlightening ASEAN (Association of Southeast Asian Nations) countries.

AUNG SAN SUU KYI'S G.S.

Japan must become the leader of ASEAN and do... The UN will not take action, so Japan should put together something with the ASEAN nations... Australia is cooperative, so Australia, Japan, and India should take the main role and also ask for support from the West. It would be best if Japan shows its willingness to take initiative and asks the U.S. and the U.K. for support, thereby strengthening alliances with them and getting backup.

Regarding the Hong Kong issue, the U.K. has dispatched naval ships while Germany announced they will also send a naval frigate there. Even Germany, a country which has never done something like that out of regret that Hitler invaded other countries, will send a frigate.

I would really be grateful if Japan would think more about peace in Asia and realizing proactive peace.

She appreciates Japan's work in WWII that put an end to European colonial rule

AUNG SAN SUU KYI'S G.S.

Although Japan was defeated in the previous world war, I appreciate Japan's work that put an end to the European colonial rule. Actually, I do.

C

I think your remark will have a positive effect on Japan in many ways.

AUNG SAN SUU KYI'S G.S.

I do appreciate it. Asian people as well... African people, or black people, were also discriminated as having no soul, and their countries were occupied one after another. White people called Asian people "yellow monkeys," so there were lots of resistance movements. Japanese people were really strong during the first two years of the war. They fought under the slogan of liberating colonies and drove away Western countries in no time. Even MacArthur was driven out of the Philippines and barely escaped to Australia.

The U.S. was a country that Japan could not win in a drawn-out war, and Italy and Germany were a bit too weak.

But Japan was trying to rebuild Asian countries and make them good countries like Taiwan, instead of aiming to colonize and rule them. So, Japan had a different attitude from the West. This is why it is a pity that Japan lost the war. I think that there might have been a path that allowed us to develop together as Buddhist countries.

C

Yes. I think your remark will have quite an impact on Japan.

Japan and India should become permanent members of the UN

AUNG SAN SUU KYI'S G.S.

Please come to help us. Japan might not have enough power as it is to fight a fierce battle against China, but the JSDF is enough to drive away Myanmar's military. So, please dispatch them.

C

I think the military would be intimidated if they saw JS Izumo or JS Kaga offshore.

AUNG SAN SUU KYI'S G.S.

They would tremble just at the sight of the JSDF. Asian people all know the Japanese forces are strong. Just the presence of the JSDF would terrify them. And, it would be better to maintain good relationship with the West and gain their support.

The UN needs to be reformed. The UN does not function at all as China and Russia both are permanent members. So, Japan and India should become permanent members.

"Japan pays more respect to our human rights than the West does"

B

Historically, your father, General Aung San, established Burma's independence with the support of the Japanese army. So, I think you could expect more from Japan than the West to help you.

AUNG SAN SUU KYI'S G.S.

Right. Japan is definitely better. Japan pays more respect to our human rights and has a better understanding of

Buddhism. Myanmar's barefoot monks look like primitive men to China, so it thinks nothing of killing all of them.

C

That's right. Exactly the same situation is now going on in Taiwan.

AUNG SAN SUU KYI'S G.S.

I see.

C

The same kind of thing is happening not only in Taiwan, but also in Myanmar and other countries you mentioned earlier. So Japan, an Asian superpower, must bear responsibility regarding this.

AUNG SAN SUU KYI'S G.S.

Yes. Japanese people, as well as some Americans, think they have no choice but to take advantage of China's economic growth to restore their economy or create another economic boom. But Japanese people must have a sense of right and wrong or a sense of justice. Otherwise, they are not qualified as a leader. They do not express their notion of good and wrong or notion of justice.

Taiwan had been exporting more than 90 percent of its pineapples to China, but China recently imposed a ban on the import of Taiwan pineapples citing it discovered pests. Then, the U.S. bought the pineapples from Taiwan. American politicians put those pineapples on their desks, indicating their stance on the matter. But this is not happening in Japan. Really, Japanese people always try to turn the situation to their advantage in many ways by not clearly stating their intention. I want a leader with the ability to tell right from wrong and a sense of justice to appear.

Her view on the Rohingya issue

A

You mentioned, "Buddhist country" several times, so I would like to ask you about the Rohingya issue.

AUNG SAN SUU KYI'S G.S.

This is difficult. Really difficult. Very difficult.

A

The Rohingya people are Muslim and refugees. I think you could have anticipated that accepting them would lead to poor security in your country.

AUNG SAN SUU KYI'S G.S.
That's true.

A

You, a Nobel Peace Prize laureate, did not do anything about that. I think some people may have campaigned against you regarding that. Could you tell us what you truly think?

AUNG SAN SUU KYI'S G.S.
The issue of Islam is a world-level problem. Now, there are conflicts in the world: one is "China vs. democratic countries" and another is "Islamic countries vs. Christian countries." The latter is also a world-level conflict. This is not a problem that Myanmar can solve alone.

India, a former Buddhist country, worships polytheistic Hinduism, so it is tolerant of other religions. However, Pakistan, a Muslim country, has no tolerance. Even Gandhi was killed because he did not agree with the independence of Pakistan.

So, Islam's lack of tolerance is quite terrible. I think Muslim nations must become more tolerant in order to have the international community accept them. Muslim immigrants have flooded European countries such as France, Germany, and the U.K., and are causing lots of problems.

Their way of thinking is outdated. Islam is a "newer religion" than Christianity, but it is outdated. Muslims try to push through an old way of thinking that was common one thousand several hundred years ago. They have too much of a fundamentalist idea.

The same is true of Pakistan. The Nobel Peace Prize laureate Ms. Malala, who went to the U.K., was once attacked while riding on the school bus, by people who believed that girls attending school is wrong according to fundamental Islam. She was shot in the head and medically transferred to the U.K., and following her recovery, she became a prominent political activist.

Islamic fundamentalists say allowing girls to attend school itself goes against Islamic teachings. Does God really teach such a thing? It probably comes from human interpretation of the teachings. Such male-centered society is rather close to military dictatorship, in some meaning. The problem of Islam is more than what I can deal with, so I would like you, Happy Science, to deal with it.

The Rohingya issue is difficult. It will lead to another civil war in our country. Every country has difficulty dealing with Muslim immigrants. I know the situation in Europe. The hard part comes after they enter the country. Muslims do not try to change their way of thinking at all. They won't accept "When in Rome, do as the Romans do." They only stick to their way of thinking. They need to be a little more...

Now is the time for Allah to send His voice from heaven. Really. I feel sorry for the Rohingya, but they... The Japanese government is trying to protect the Rohingya, but it is quite difficult to provide a place for them.

B
I understand.

5

The Secret of Ms. Aung San Suu Kyi's Soul

What is lacking in Myanmar's (Burma's) Buddhism?

B

Later on, we would like to hear from the guardian spirit of Senior General Hlaing who led the coup, if possible.

I have another question, if you don't mind me asking. Since you are a Buddhist, and Burma or Myanmar is a Buddhist-majority country, you are seeking for Buddha to save you. Do you, the guardian spirit of Ms. Aung San Suu Kyi, have some connection with Buddhism or a special bond with Buddha?

AUNG SAN SUU KYI'S G.S.

Hinayana Buddhism is too this-worldly religion. It tends to focus too much on discipline. It mainly encourages an individual to get closer to Buddha through meditation, so believers are not so good at acting in groups or creating a society. Even if monks try to stage a mass demonstration, they do not know how because Buddha preached very few teachings on politics. India, in fact, has been tossed about by political confusion.

Mahayana Buddhism has interacted with politics in many ways, while Hinayana Buddhism has distanced itself from politics and urged individuals to devote themselves to discipline. That being said, in Burma, monks are the ones that are revered by the people. There is no longer Buddha or Dharma, but only Sangha in Burma. There is no "Dharma" that teaches us how to deal with this situation. There are temples and Buddha statues for worship, but people do not understand what lies beyond them. The spiritual aspect is lacking in Myanmar's Buddhism, and some magical elements of folk religions or shamanism were incorporated into it. People still curse others to death. This kind of shamanism complements the weakness of Myanmar's Buddhism.

Her feelings for Buddhism and expectations for Happy Science

AUNG SAN SUU KYI'S G.S.

Personally, I think Buddhism is a religion of peace, tolerance, and non-discrimination. I think this is a very good aspect of Buddhism in the worldly sense.

However, because Buddhism is not so positive about military matters, many Buddhist countries were destroyed. The reason Buddhism perished in India is that Muslims attacked and destroyed Buddhist temples and killed all the monks. The two religions have a history.

What does Buddha think of this? Buddhism perished in India when Muslims invaded the country in 1203, killing all monks and destroying all temples and Buddha statues. They will do the same thing in Myanmar and Thailand. They will ultimately destroy temples and Buddha statues in both countries.

What does Buddha think? What does he think of the military? I think the only religion who can offer answers to these questions is Happy Science. So, do not be afraid to come to our country to spread your teachings. We have monks, but they lack intelligence, so they cannot answer these questions.

A

When the living Ms. Suu Kyi came to Japan, the students of Happy Science directly handed her an English translation of *The Laws of Future*. So, please give her your inspiration.

AUNG SAN SUU KYI'S G.S.

She may not be able to live so long and I do not think she could help you, but I can say that if you do not raise the level of Buddhism, we are done for.

C

You said she may not be able to live long. We will work hard to enlighten the world, so we hope she will hang on a bit longer.

AUNG SAN SUU KYI'S G.S.

I am not sure whether it is house arrest or confinement, but my life has been full of being captured and "sealed." So, I do not know how old my intelligence is now.

C

I do not know whether it is good to cite Mr. Mandela as an example, but...

AUNG SAN SUU KYI'S G.S.

Ah, uh-huh.

C

The fact that there was a person that persevered through adversity served as a strong unifying force.

AUNG SAN SUU KYI'S G.S.

If there is anyone who can help us, we don't really care who it is, be it Happy Science or whatever.

"I was born in Japan during the Kamakura period"

B

This is a question from the spiritual point of view. You are now living in the same age as Master Ryuho Okawa and are a leader of a Buddhist country. I am not sure if you know the answer to this question, but did you have any connection with Shakyamuni Buddha?

AUNG SAN SUU KYI'S G.S.

Hmm. Well, something is wrong with Hinayana Buddhism. All of you might laugh when you hear this, but as you know, there are the teachings of "impermanence of all things," "egolessness of all phenomena," and "perfect tranquility of nirvana." In Hinayana Buddhism, "perfect tranquility of nirvana" means that when people who become Buddha pass away to the other world, they perish and enter the state of no thoughts. It's uncertain if they exist or not. These teachings make people unintelligent. Something is wrong with them.

I know I am a guardian spirit, a spirit, but monks do not even know what a guardian spirit is. That is why a folk belief or something like black magic is still popular among the people. Shamans perform their work clearly recognizing the existence of spirits.

So, Buddhism has a defect. Buddhist people are revered because they live a moral life and are pure, but they are ignorant of the Truth in some meaning.

As for me, I am in Myanmar now, but I was born in other countries. I was once born in Japan, too.

C
In what period?

AUNG SAN SUU KYI'S G.S.
During the Kamakura period.

C

The Kamakura period? Is that so?

AUNG SAN SUU KYI'S G.S.

Yes, yes. The Kamakura period.

C

Could you be more specific?

AUNG SAN SUU KYI'S G.S.

Well, it's... Hmm.

B

Is there anyone you know from that period?

AUNG SAN SUU KYI'S G.S.

I am not sure, but the Minamoto clan came into power, you know? They were working hard to establish the Shogunate. At that time, there was a woman named Masako Hojo. It is said that she was a nun, but she couldn't have become one by herself; there was a Buddhist nunnery. I was also one of the nuns in a nunnery temple during the Kamakura period, so I knew her.

This is why I have come to ask for help; I have some connection with your religion. I think Japan has enough strength to repel foreign countries. You could find out my name if you do the research, but I was really, really, a no-name. I was not a big name. A no-name in Japan could become a big name in Burma. There is a difference in the levels of the two countries. I hope Japan will fight well like when it defeated the Yuan.

Ms. Suu Kyi's past lives in India and Britain

AUNG SAN SUU KYI'S G.S.
I was born as a Japanese as well as an Indian.

C
During what period in India were you born?

AUNG SAN SUU KYI'S G.S.
I was born slightly later than Shakyamuni Buddha's time. That is, I was born in the period when Buddhism was spreading and Nalanda University was growing big with as many as 10,000 students. And, I was also born in Europe.

C

Could you tell us about that?

AUNG SAN SUU KYI'S G.S.

Huh?

C

About the time when you were born in Europe.

AUNG SAN SUU KYI'S G.S.

Regarding Europe, I have some connection with Britain. I was born in the Kamakura period and at the time of Nalanda, but in between them, I had another life in Britain. I think it was around the time of King Arthur. I was one of those who served in the court.

At that time, Celtic religion, not Christianity, was still prevalent in Britain. The name Odin (the Principal God in Norse Mythology) was still famous. Odin loved poetry and music very much, and I was dealing with religious poems and music in the court.

She requests the JSDF be dispatched
under the pretext of protecting Japanese citizens

B

Thank you for giving us valuable messages.

AUNG SAN SUU KYI'S G.S.

Japan, please come to help us.

B

Yes.

A

Happy Science is going to spread a song called "The Water Revolution" (See p. 196) throughout Asia as well as the world and overturn the Chinese oppression through "Power to the People."

AUNG SAN SUU KYI'S G.S.

Hmm, I prefer "The Yangon Revolution" or "The Burmese Revolution" or "The Harp Keeps Playing"[2] instead of "The Water Revolution." We need you to shift more of your attention to us.

Anyway, Beijing is behind the scenes. It definitely is. So, do not succumb to China. Contain China instead of being contained.

There is not much I can do. The only thing I can do is to spiritually ask you for help and send out the message that we have hope in Japan. That is all I can do.

I would like the Japanese army to take over. Please come to help us. The Burmese army is weak. It would take the JSDF a week at most to defeat them all. Please come to help us, I really mean it. The UN will never come. Never. China will veto, and that will be the end of the story.

B

We understand you put great hopes on Japan. Today's message will surely reach the Japanese people.

AUNG SAN SUU KYI'S G.S.

There are Japanese citizens still in Myanmar, so please come to protect them.

C

Under the pretext of protecting Japanese citizens in Myanmar. I see.

AUNG SAN SUU KYI'S G.S.

Please come to help us.

B

I understand. OK.

AUNG SAN SUU KYI'S G.S.

Japan is too weak. In reality, it is much stronger than you might think. The JSDF has not been doing much. It is just protecting Japanese tankers from pirate attacks in the Strait of Hormuz, that's all. We are closer to your country, so please dispatch them.

I want to build an alliance with Japan again. We are in serious danger unless we form an alliance with a country other than China. China is constructing a high-speed railway from Yunnan Province through Southeast Asia and planning to rule the entire region. It intends to take control of India, too, by constructing the railway.

If this continues, I cannot die in peace.

B

Your message today will definitely reach the Japanese people.

AUNG SAN SUU KYI'S G.S.

I count on you.

B

Yes. Thank you.

"What matters in politics is philosophy" "You must teach people the direction they should head"

AUNG SAN SUU KYI'S G.S.

Your religion is involved in politics, right?

B

Yes.

AUNG SAN SUU KYI'S G.S.

So, you need a little more... Making money is not enough. Politics is not only about making money. What matters in politics is philosophy. It is about how you think of things and about showing the path. This is what politics is all about.

You must show people the path and teach them the direction they should head. You must do this as Japanese people.

B

Thank you for having hope in us. After this session, we will hear from the opposing side...

AUNG SAN SUU KYI'S G.S.

Oh, is that so?

B

Yes, from Senior General Hlaing.

AUNG SAN SUU KYI'S G.S.

Yes, yes.

B

We want to confirm with him.

AUNG SAN SUU KYI'S G.S.

That's all from me. I am a little drained. I am an old lady, after all. If only I were 20 years younger, I would still do more. But I cannot anymore. Mr. Trump would be willing to do more, but it is tough for me.

B

OK. We definitely got your message.

AUNG SAN SUU KYI'S G.S.

This might be my "dying message." Yes. OK.

B

OK. Thank you very much.

6

Myanmar Suffers from Lack of Capable Leaders

RYUHO OKAWA

[*Claps twice.*] That's it. I think she is a pro-Japanese, so I feel sorry for her. She is probably the best-known Burmese among Japanese people.

B

Right.

RYUHO OKAWA

The country does not have capable leaders besides Ms. Suu Kyi. Unfortunately, there is no other capable person, I mean, a charismatic or iconic figure. I feel sorry for her. I really do.

The military thinks she won't be able to exert any influence as long as she is under house arrest and without information. It is similar to the blocking of information (against Mr. Trump) in the U.S.

TRANSLATOR'S NOTE

1 *Kuro-Obi Eigo* (lit. "Black Belt English") is an English textbook series published by Happy Science for Japanese people who want to study English.

2 There is a famous Japanese novel titled, *Harp of Burma*.

CHAPTER TWO

The Truth about the Coup and China's True Aim

Spiritual Interview with the Guardian Spirit of General Min Aung Hlaing

*Originally recorded in Japanese on March 11, 2021
at the Special Lecture Hall of Happy Science in Japan
and later translated into English.*

In this chapter, there are a total of three interviewers from Happy Science, symbolized as A, B, and C, in the order that they first appear.

Min Aung Hlaing (1956 – Present)

A Burmese army general, politician, and the commander-in-chief of Defence Services. He studied law at the Rangoon Arts and Science University (now the University Yangon), and was admitted to the Defence Services Academy in 1974. In 2007, he supported the military crackdown on the Saffron Revolution, an anti-government movement led by monks. He led an offensive against the insurgents since 2008, and for this achievement, rose to the commander-in-chief of Defence Services in 2011. In 2017, the UN called for his prosecution regarding the genocide against Rohingya Muslims. On February 1, 2021, he launched a coup claiming that the results of the country's general election in November 2020 were fraudulent.

1

Why Did Myanmar's Military Launch a Coup?

Summoning the guardian spirit of Senior General Hlaing, who led the coup

RYUHO OKAWA

The army general we want to interview next also likes social media platforms like Facebook. But he is blocking out a lot of information now, so we will have to see how this interview will work out.

B

Yes. If you do not mind, I would like to simply hear the opinions of the guardian spirit of Senior General Hlaing, who led the coup.

RYUHO OKAWA

He seems to be around my age. Shall we give it a try? He is small in stature and seems to be a good-natured person, but he is getting along well with China. He also claims that Myanmar's election on November 8, 2020 was rigged. I am not quite sure. I do not know if I can talk with him.

[*Puts hands in prayer and closes eyes.*]

General Min Aung Hlaing, General Min Aung Hlaing, General Min Aung Hlaing. Could you come down here? This is Happy Science, Tokyo, Japan. General Hlaing. Hlaing, Hlaing, Hlaing... Can you talk to us?

"Military personnel also have a retirement age" "I staged the coup to create work"

MIN AUNG HLAING'S G.S.
Ah, umm, ah... Umm... ah... Umm, umm, umm, umm. Ah, umm, ah, ah... Umm, umm... Umm, ah... Umm. [*Raises right hand.*] Ah...

B
Hello.

MIN AUNG HLAING'S G.S.

One... One, word by word, in an easy way...

B

OK. I will speak slowly.

MIN AUNG HLAING'S G.S.

I can understand your feelings.

B

OK. I will ask some simple questions. Are you the guardian spirit of Senior General Hlaing?

MIN AUNG HLAING'S G.S.

Yes.

B

OK. The coup occurred in Myanmar. What was your purpose and what are you thinking now? What are you going to do with Myanmar?

MIN AUNG HLAING'S G.S.

Umm... Military personnel have a retirement age, too. If we quit, we will have no job. But if I establish a military government, we can work.

C

I heard that you were near retirement age.

MIN AUNG HLAING'S G.S.

Yes, yes. So, I staged a coup to create work.

B

Do you have a purpose or an ideal to contribute to Myanmar?

MIN AUNG HLAING'S G.S.

No, I do not.

B

You don't?!

MIN AUNG HLAING'S G.S.

Umm. No, I don't. But it is not good to have monks and citizens riot and destabilize the country, so I thought we should govern it.

B

The crackdown on demonstrations against military rule resulted in civilian deaths. Do you think this is the right thing to do?

MIN AUNG HLAING'S G.S.
We did not kill *everyone*. It's just several or a several dozen people, you know? If it were a massacre, we would have to kill more than 10,000 people, but we refrained from going that far. The police is under military control, so police chiefs are also military officers.

Public security comes first. If the level of public security drops, there is no knowing what might happen. If we are able to restore stability, we will be able to implement economic policies. People can live. Uh-huh.

"China occupies half of the world, so I thought the survival of our country would be guaranteed"

C
It is said that there was a close coordination or arrangements between you and China. Could you tell us about that?

MIN AUNG HLAING'S G.S.
Of course, there was. We could not have staged a coup otherwise.

C

Specifically, what arrangements did you make?

MIN AUNG HLAING'S G.S.

China said, "Min Aung Hlaing, you should rule Myanmar," or something like that.

C

If you rule Myanmar, what will China do for you?

MIN AUNG HLAING'S G.S.

Huh? It means China will provide us with a strong backup. They will not only offer us economic assistance, but also help us with the development of urban infrastructure and high-speed railway system, and help us become a highly developed country.

C

Other Asian countries have been deceived by China's sweet talk and are now having their property confiscated or taken away on many occasions. What are your thoughts on this?

MIN AUNG HLAING'S G.S.

Our country already gained independence from the U.K. We will not have the U.K. rule us again. We refuse that. China is now the most powerful country. It occupies half the world, so I thought the survival of our country will be guaranteed.

A

The coup occurred in February because the military claimed the election to be fraudulent.

MIN AUNG HLAING'S G.S.

I hate elections to begin with.

A

Did you receive the direction from China about when to launch the coup?

MIN AUNG HLAING'S G.S.

Umm... I am not sure, but China wanted to cause some confusion. It happened around the time of the U.S. presidential election. So, I guess so?

C

Could you be more specific about it? I mean, regarding "China wanted to cause some confusion."

MIN AUNG HLAING'S G.S.

Umm... About 30 million Americans or 1 in 10 Americans are infected by the coronavirus (at the time of this spiritual interview). They wouldn't be able to do anything, so we thought it was a good time for us to carry out a coup.

2

China's Outlook as Heard by the Guardian Spirit of Hlaing

He believes Tibet became rich because it exiled the Dalai Lama

B

If your move has been backed by China, it is likely that they will eventually take over your country economically or that your country will be ruined. What do you think of Xi Jinping?

MIN AUNG HLAING'S G.S.

Actually, China used to be the center of the world many times, so if it tells us to pay tributes, we will. You know? I do not mind doing that, if we are given something in return.

C

I mean, for example, China killed many people in Tibet and took over the region despite the fact that Tibet paid some tributes. Don't you fear that this might happen to your country?

MIN AUNG HLAING'S G.S.

It was said that Tibetan Buddhism was corrupted. "His Holiness" Dalai Lama was an autocracy, and he had control over religion, politics, and economy. The Chinese People's Liberation Army fought against the autocracy to "liberate" Tibetan people and drove out the monks, or the exploiting class, to India. So, Tibet is now enjoying a better economy.

Thanks to the high-speed railway system making it all the way into the Tibet Autonomous Region, the economic growth rate of Tibet is higher compared to any other region in China. They are enjoying the greatest prosperity. I heard that thanks to the exile of Dalai Lama, Tibetans have become affluent and their level of education has been raised.

China: "Vietnam is unforgivable" "There is a sign of rebellion in North Korea"

C

Perhaps Xi Jinping told you about China's outlook in a series of talks you had with him immediately before the coup and a year ago, and they probably were not just about Myanmar or Burma alone. What are your thoughts on that?

MIN AUNG HLAING'S G.S.

OK. He said China is extremely displeased that Vietnam, which is supposed to be a communist country, is getting closer to the U.S. China supported Vietnam's independence and helped it militarily and economically to drive out the U.S. from Saigon. China cannot forgive Vietnam because even though it dispatched its voluntary army to Vietnam to fight and kick the U.S. out in exchange for a number of casualties, Vietnam forgot how much it owes to China and is buttering up to the U.S.

China cannot forgive the fact that Vietnam is implementing U.S.-style economic reform and open-door policies. Kim Jong-un of North Korea says he wants to bring the country closer to the U.S., and China sees it as a sign of rebellion. Xi Jinping intends to take over both North Korea and South Korea, but since Trump met with Kim Jong-un in person, there is a possibility that he will run to Trump if China invades North Korea. Xi said that battles were happening simultaneously in many places.

What is China planning to do with Thailand, Malaysia, and Indonesia?

C

How about Thailand?

MIN AUNG HLAING'S G.S.

China is conducting many acts of espionage in Thailand where the military dictatorship, democracy, and monarchy are fighting each other. Xi said China could possibly take over Thailand if it can take control of Myanmar.

C

If China takes control of Thailand, then Malaysia will be next.

MIN AUNG HLAING'S G.S.

Xi said he intended to make all neighboring countries Chinese territory and make Chinese their official language.

C

Indonesia is a major power among the Southeast Asian countries. Did he mention...

MIN AUNG HLAING'S G.S.

It is difficult to take over Indonesia because of religious problems, that is, it is an Islamic nation.

China and Japan are competing for Indonesia because it has oil fields. China has its eyes on Indonesia. Hmm... Its population is increasing now, so China is concerned about whether it should let Indonesia be a powerhouse.

China said it was capturing Muslim countries. It said something like, "The Western countries are now retreating from fossil fuels such as oil and coal in an effort to decarbonize, so now is the time when China can take over Muslim nations in one stroke."

China's "excuse" to invade India

C

Allow me to ask you another question. Since India, Nepal, and Bhutan are relatively close to Myanmar, you two probably talked about those countries. Could you share something about that?

MIN AUNG HLAING'S G.S.
India, Nepal, Bhutan... Actually, China is plotting to invade India.

C
Is it plotting an invasion?

MIN AUNG HLAING'S G.S.
It is planning to invade from the north. Dalai Lama established the Tibetan government in exile in India, so China will attack India under the pretext of a pursuit battle. That will be China's "excuse."

Bhutan will be brought under China's control soon. China said that if we worked hard, we could be a part of China and establish the Great Chinese Empire.

C
I understand.

3

Dealing with the Resistance by Burmese People

"Democracy is wrong" "Western countries must be excluded"

C

Let us get back to the problems in Myanmar. I understand what you said, but on the other hand, Burmese people have experienced democracy and freedom for about 10 years, although they were with restrictions. What is your take on that? People's resistance...

MIN AUNG HLAING'S G.S.

It's very... Democracy does not match our country. It does not match our faith, the Buddhist faith, either. When you see the monks marching in red robes, you will know that they are like the army. So, Buddhism and army go well with each other. I think the military should take control in Myanmar, Laos, Thailand, and other countries around there.

C

Let us leave aside the debate over whether the Sangha is democratic or not, and...

MIN AUNG HLAING'S G.S.
Actually, the Sangha is...

C

Sangha, meaning the Buddhist order.

MIN AUNG HLAING'S G.S.
Actually, the Sangha is not democratic, but totalitarian.

C

We won't discuss about its interpretation today. Anyway, what I wanted to ask you was, from the perspective of an outsider, the resistance of the people when the coup occurred is stronger than expected and is still going on.

MIN AUNG HLAING'S G.S.
People who have enjoyed "greedy democracy" are saying they want to make money however they want. Buddhist ascetic training is to abandon those desires. So, democracy is wrong. The Western countries must be excluded.

Hlaing's model is Cambodia— purging intellectuals who returned from abroad

B

Incidentally, the guardian spirit of Ms. Suu Kyi was here earlier. How do you see her? She has been working hard for a long time as a pro-democracy leader.

MIN AUNG HLAING'S G.S.

She is not suitable for a pro-democratic leader. She rose to power just because she is the daughter of a general. It is blood lineage. She is not like me, who seized power through my skills.

C

That is how you look at her. Anyway, here is my question. Historically, in countries around China, there were dictators like you...

MIN AUNG HLAING'S G.S.

Umm. I am not a dictator.

C

Or, "powerful leaders," and when they joined forces with the Chinese Communist government to become its satellite nation that is almost like an autonomous region, in most cases, they heavily oppressed the people and put many of them in a very miserable situation. There is such a "pattern" of history.

MIN AUNG HLAING'S G.S.
Hmm.

C

It seems to me that the history of your country is moving in that direction. Aren't you concerned about this?

MIN AUNG HLAING'S G.S.
Cambodia is a good example. All intellectuals that returned from abroad should be "hunted," I mean, purging all intellectuals will lead to peace in the country.

C

Then, you also want to do the same for Myanmar, to get rid of them once?

MIN AUNG HLAING'S G.S.

Yes. So, Suu Kyi is the very first person we must kill. But we cannot kill her for fear of international criticism, so we have only placed her under house arrest.

C

You think that way at a subconscious level.

MIN AUNG HLAING'S G.S.

We do not need people who studied in the U.K. like her in Myanmar. That is not what we need. The common people's standard of living is a bit lower, so they need a way of thinking that matches them.

C

Perhaps you could call it "happiness of slaves"...

MIN AUNG HLAING'S G.S.

She learned aristocratic tastes in Britain. But this country will never be like that because our only industry is agriculture.

A

You mean, you do not mind carrying out a massacre against your people like the Pol Pot regime in Cambodia and creating the Killing Fields?

MIN AUNG HLAING'S G.S.

"Massacre" might not be the right word. After all, we have to "dispose of" those who do not obey us.

His views on Buddhism and monks, and his awareness as a spirit

MIN AUNG HLAING'S G.S.

I think Buddhism and monks are important. I can accept totalitarian Buddhism that becomes a pawn of the military and teaches the people to obey the government. But if Buddhism becomes individualistic or political that encourages monks to protest, it is corrupted.

C

Your views on Buddhism perfectly match those of the Chinese Communist Party.

MIN AUNG HLAING'S G.S.

Those who do not pay taxes and live only on offerings should be rounded up and drowned into the sea.

B

We are running out of time, so let me ask you one last question. Are you aware that you are a guardian spirit or a spiritual being?

MIN AUNG HLAING'S G.S.

What? No, I'm not.

B

Oh, you aren't?

MIN AUNG HLAING'S G.S.

I don't know about that. I don't really know.

B

Is there anyone who interacts with you, or gives you directions or orders?

MIN AUNG HLAING'S G.S.

What? Hmm, hmm. Ah. Well, I don't really know about that.

B

You don't know?

MIN AUNG HLAING'S G.S.

I don't really know, but I came here because you summoned me. I don't really know. I don't really know why I can have a conversation with you.

B

We are talking in Japan now.

MIN AUNG HLAING'S G.S.

I don't really understand that.

B

OK. We understand.

MIN AUNG HLAING'S G.S.

What? I don't understand how this works. This is my first time.

4

Responding to International Criticisms

Would the most intelligent people form an alliance with China?

C

At the beginning of the interview, you said you launched the coup to postpone your retirement.

MIN AUNG HLAING'S G.S.

It would be a waste not to use a competent person like me. I am more than 10 years younger than Suu Kyi.

C

OK. With the motive of that level, would you be able to withstand the pressure, sanctions, and opinions of the international society, which are expected to get quite tough?

MIN AUNG HLAING'S G.S.

Xi Jinping says, "With the Biden administration, you do not have to worry," and "Japan is weak and will readily recognize the military government." So, I think I will be OK.

C

You think that way.

MIN AUNG HLAING'S G.S.

Yes. The Western countries are far from us. They cannot do much. We have already received food and military support, so there is no need to worry now.

C

But that means China has control over Myanmar's lifeline, which means they can choose to let you live or die.

MIN AUNG HLAING'S G.S.

Obviously, it is just a matter of time before China becomes the world's number one country. It will become the world's number one in the 2020s.

So, if we form an alliance with China and make developments in Myanmar, people's lives will be better, and it will also serve as a deterrent to foreign military forces. This is what the most intelligent people would do.

Are monks and temples no longer necessary?

C

The leaders of the military government can benefit from the alliance with China, but the general public would fall into dire straits like the people in North Korea. Do you envision such a future?

MIN AUNG HLAING'S G.S.

All monks should be secularized and made to work. They should be a taxi driver or whatever. They should work. That would increase the tax revenue.

C

You mean, you want Myanmar to be a non-religious country.

MIN AUNG HLAING'S G.S.

Yes. They are unnecessary. We don't need them, really. The people are "doubly taxed" because of them.

Taxes are necessary to support the military personnel. We need taxes to support the police and even monks... monks individually collect taxes and live off it, so we do not need them. We do not need temples, either. We will consider leaving them if we can use them for tourism and if they can earn revenues only from tourism.

A

Don't you ever think what would happen to you in the afterlife?

MIN AUNG HLAING'S G.S.

I don't know about that.

He justifies military dictatorship

B

We got a rough idea of how you think. Thank you.

MIN AUNG HLAING'S G.S.

So, Japan... If we show a strong attitude, then Japan or Japan's Foreign Ministry will easily give us money. It will give money in exchange for the protection of Japanese citizens living in Myanmar. That is all Japan has.

B

Thank you for giving us a valuable message.

MIN AUNG HLAING'S G.S.

There is nothing Japan can do. Japan isn't a problem at all.

C

We will have to see what happens from now on.

B

Now that the topic of Buddhism, politics, and democracy came up, I would like to wrap up this interview here.

MIN AUNG HLAING'S G.S.

Is it all right with you?

B

Yes, it is.

MIN AUNG HLAING'S G.S.

The reason why we allow Suu Kyi to live is that the West will criticize us. If we kill her, we will come under criticisms, so we have no choice but to let her die slowly.

It is not good for a ruling political party to change so often depending on the outcome of the election. In addition, the military is not so good at party politics, so we do not want that. The government should not sway so much.

We are now encouraging Thailand's military to rule the country. Military dictatorship will make the country most stable. Beijing also says that military dictatorship can bring long-term stability to the country and make it easier to make a long-term plan.

B

Hearing your views, we understand very clearly what we are against.

MIN AUNG HLAING'S G.S.

Oh, really?

B

Yes. Thank you.

MIN AUNG HLAING'S G.S.

There is no point asking that old Suu Kyi. You will never be able to see her. She will leave this world soon. Oh, yes she will.

His views on Buddhism and politics reveal his level as a person

MIN AUNG HLAING'S G.S.

So, what was this today?

B

Buddhism is one of the basic themes, so we would like to ask Shakyamuni Buddha for his message next, if he is OK with it.

MIN AUNG HLAING'S G.S.

There is no such thing. What are you saying?

C

Are you afraid of what he would say?

MIN AUNG HLAING'S G.S.

He died more than 2,500 years ago. What can he say?

C

You are afraid of him, aren't you?

MIN AUNG HLAING'S G.S.

No, no. There can be no such thing.

C

You are afraid since you said you are going to kill monks.

MIN AUNG HLAING'S G.S.

Monks? Monks live on the old teachings that were preached 2,500 years ago. We don't need them. They are useless, good-for-nothings. We do not need them anymore. They are cockroaches or flies.

C

We understand that you are feeling quite uneasy.

B

There is a Buddhist term, *mappo* ("final Dharma"). We understand your views go completely against religion.

MIN AUNG HLAING'S G.S.

Hmm... Well, it is best we rule the country. We will develop like China.

B

Thank you for your opinions.

RYUHO OKAWA

[*Claps twice.*] He is a person of this level. I think it is low, very low. I expected him to be so. His level is low. It is. I think he is uncivilized.

CHAPTER THREE

Summing up the Myanmar Problem

Spiritual Messages from Shakyamuni Buddha

*Originally recorded in Japanese on on March 11, 2021
at the Special Lecture Hall of Happy Science in Japan
and later translated into English.*

In this chapter, the interviewer is symbolized as B.

Shakyamuni Buddha
(Gautama Siddhartha)

The founder of Buddhism, who was born about 2,500 or 2,600 years ago in the area now known as Nepal. He was born to *Suddhodana*, the king of the *Shakya* clan, who ruled a nearby kingdom called *Kapilavastu*, and the queen *Maya*. Although he was raised as a prince, he renounced the world at the age of 29 to seek after the truth and attained Great Enlightenment at the age of 35. After performing the first preaching (the First Turning of the Wheel of Truth) at the Deer Park or *Magadaava*, he continued to preach the law throughout India until he died at the age of 80. After his death, Buddhism became a world religion. *Shakyamuni* is an abbreviation of *Shakyamuni bhagavat* (the honorary name meaning "World-Honored One of the *Shakya* clan").

1

Asking Shakyamuni Buddha to Sum up the Myanmar Problem

"I hope we will be able to spread the Buddhist spirit that includes prosperity and progress"

B

If possible, could we ask Shakyamuni Buddha to give us words to sum up the Myanmar problem, even if it's brief?

RYUHO OKAWA

Oh, all right.

Gautama Siddhartha, Shakyamuni Buddha.

Gautama Siddhartha, Shakyamuni Buddha.

We would appreciate it if you could share your views on Myanmar or Burma with us.

[*About five seconds of silence.*]

SHAKYAMUNI BUDDHA

Yes.

B

Today, we summoned the guardian spirits of Ms. Suu Kyi and General Hlaing, and heard their opinions. The topics of Buddhism, politics, and democracy came up, so we would really appreciate it if you could sum up today's session.

SHAKYAMUNI BUDDHA

Buddhism perished in India and China, and it is also perishing in Japan. It cannot be helped in the great course of history, so we are now trying to establish a new religion.

We can do nothing to stop that, but our work now is to establish a new religion instead. So, I hope we will be able to spread the Buddhist spirit that includes prosperity and progress.

Both Myanmar and Thailand need to be rebuilt, including a religious reform

SHAKYAMUNI BUDDHA

I think things are really tough in Myanmar. You are talking about "military rule" and "democracy," but there is another issue. That is, both sides believe that faith is useless. Democratic countries think science is almighty, while military regimes try to exploit faith where they can, although they have no interest in faith. After all, I think a new religion that replaces Buddhism, Christianity, and Islam is needed now.

I am thinking about what we can do with this region. When Myanmar was in turmoil before, a cyclone struck the country and displaced great numbers of people. Catastrophic natural disasters happen not only in Japan, but also in these regions.

We are now discussing what we should do. We think we should not abandon a country that has Buddhist temples and many monks, but it is doubtful whether people in Myanmar as well as Thailand believe in Buddha these days. If those people have become an existing force and steadfastly refuse to accept new teachings, I think we have no choice but to let them take their course, but even so, I would like to start a reformation movement.

Similarly, things are tough in Thailand. Buddhism has permeated in Thailand, but the king has replaced God and gained control of the military. Some people there feel they are training themselves spiritually by becoming a temporary monk and experiencing a monastic life, but it is almost like experiencing Zen meditation in Eihei-ji Temple or practicing asking for alms. They aren't able to reach the world of essential religious enlightenment, and Thailand also has a lot of crime.

Therefore, those countries need to be rebuilt, including a religious reform. Such a way of thinking is required. So, I would like Happy Science to get into those countries as much as possible. You may not want to do that because you will just end up spending money, but I would like you to use your abilities to help those Buddhist countries reform themselves.

Mahayana Buddhism teaches "each individual has Buddha-nature," which accords with democracy

SHAKYAMUNI BUDDHA

That being said, there is a major battle you must not lose. Now, the frontline is Hong Kong and Taiwan. China denies democracy in Hong Kong.

Of course, Buddhist teachings do not completely accord with democracy, but the teachings of Mahayana Buddhism that have been handed down to the present day are based on the idea that each individual has Buddha-nature. This idea accords with democracy in the West. The objective of democracy is, after all, to pursue human happiness.

There are differing opinions over the interpretation of happiness, but China looks at happiness only as being fulfilled in the materialistic sense. If you are aware of China's motive to destroy a country like Bhutan that enjoys happiness resulting from spiritual fulfillment, you must resolutely resist it.

So, Japanese businesses should not be occupied with making money trading with China. Some Japanese businesspeople have become very rich by constructing factories in China and creating many jobs there. If you just look at their desire to make Chinese people's lives better, it is not a bad thing. They believed that raising Chinese people's standard of living and cultural level would bring China closer to Western democracy. But if that leads to military dictatorship or communist dictatorship, it will bring misfortune on the people.

The uneducated Xi Jinping's idea is an ancient rule of law, or the rule of law that is convenient for a ruler. He is trying to bind his people under such rule of law and preventing his people from thinking by blocking out information. If Japanese businesspeople think that governing a country under such rule of law means to "become prosperous," then I want to say they are wrong. Democracy includes the idea that values individual freedom and individual philosophy, and in the Buddhist sense, this is similar to each person's desire to seek the Truth. So, I would like to strike a balance and guide them in the good direction.

You must teach "spiritual revolution" to a country that only thinks about satisfying materialistic desires

SHAKYAMUNI BUDDHA

I am afraid Myanmar will be in a dire situation in the future. I would like Japan to firmly establish Japanese-style prosperity in that country. But it may be difficult as Japan is also having a hard time now.

You must not be deceived by this smoke screen laid by China. In the U.S., 30 million people have been infected by the coronavirus, while China has overcome it with about 100,000 (at the time of the recording). And, China set an economic growth target of more than six percent, while

Western countries have all experienced negative growth. This is absurd. To counter those who are attempting to control the world using such illusions, I think you need to show the reality to the people of the world.

They ignore the other world and the mind. They believe there is no such thing as the other world or the mind. All they think of is satisfying worldly, materialistic desires. So, I think it is important to teach them "spiritual revolution." Happy Science's current approach is to express your opinions first, so I think it is important to spread your teachings.

The Biden administration of the U.S. is trying to counter China, but China is always making excuses and saying that it's "foreign interference of domestic affairs" when other countries say to protect the people of Hong Kong and Taiwan or when they talk about human rights violations in Uyghur. But I must say that you must not give tremendous power to a country that refuses to let the truth be revealed.

B
Thank you very much. [*To other interviewers.*] Any other questions? No? OK.

SHAKYAMUNI BUDDHA

OK, then.

B

Thank you for sharing your valuable message with us today.

SHAKYAMUNI BUDDHA

[*Claps once.*]

2

Japan Must Take Responsibility for the World

RYUHO OKAWA

OK. Thank you. [*Claps once.*]

It was on short notice, but we mainly talked with (the guardian spirit of) Ms. Aung San Suu Kyi under the title, "Will There Be Peace in Myanmar?" Ms. Suu Kyi herself seems to be in the depths of despair, so we hope our voice from Japan will reach her.

Chief director of International Headquarters, I am not sure what we can do, but please do whatever we can do to help her. Are the Burmese who are living in Japan making protests or something? If there is something we can do to help them, please do it even if it means only spending our budget.

It is time for another change to come on the international level. We must block China's moves. We must not allow the "evil empire" to take control. We have completed the English and Chinese versions of the song, "The Water Revolution," and this will likely have an impact on China, so I think we must fight by steadily spreading it.

Especially, Japanese people's attitude of just standing by and watching seems egoistic to the outside world. What is necessary now is a leader who can make a value judgment. We must be able to send out a value judgment from Asia.

Some people may think it does not matter whether Bhutan lives happily or is taken over by China, but this must not be allowed to happen. In Myanmar, temples will be destroyed and monks will be killed under the military dictatorship, and perhaps the top of the military does not even know that those who do such things will not be accepted by the international community, so there is a need to enlighten him.

I would like Japan to become a country that can take responsibility for the world, and I believe this is one of the things Japan must do since it couldn't during the previous world war.

B
Yes. Thank you very much for today.

RYUHO OKAWA
OK.

EXTRA CHAPTER

Messages from Space Regarding the Coup in Myanmar

UFO Reading 61
(Wilmar from Planet Wilmar)

Originally recorded in Japanese on March 10, 2021
at the Special Lecture Hall of Happy Science in Japan
and later translated into English.

In this chapter, the interviewer is symbolized as A.

It is said from ancient times that those who have attained enlightenment like Shakyamuni Buddha can use abilities beyond human knowledge freely at their will, namely the Six Divine Supernatural Powers (astral travel, spiritual sight, spiritual hearing, mind reading, fate reading, and extinction of worldly desires). These spiritual abilities of the highest level transcend the boundaries of time and space, and enable one to freely see through the past, present and future lives. Okawa is able to use these Six Divine Supernatural Powers freely and conduct various readings.

In the spiritual reading sessions compiled in this book, Okawa uses these abilities to conduct spiritual messages, spiritual vision, time-travel reading (seeing through the subject's past and future), remote-viewing (sending part of the spirit body to a specific location and seeing the situation there), mind-reading (reading the subject's thoughts and will, including those in a remote location), and mutual conversation (communicating with the thoughts of various beings that are beyond human contact).

1

A Space Being Asks Happy Science to Help Myanmar

An attempt to communicate with a space being that claims to have a connection to Ms. Suu Kyi

A

OK.

RYUHO OKAWA

(Are the UFOs) Captured on the camera?

A

Yes.

RYUHO OKAWA

OK. In the sky above Minato Ward, a little past 10 PM on March 10, 2021. In which direction are they?

A

[*Looks at the camera screen.*] Wow. Amazing.

The Background That
Led to This Space People Reading

UFOs appeared in the night sky on March 10, 2021, the day before Happy Science recorded "Spiritual Interview with the Guardian Spirit of Aung San Suu Kyi - Will There Be Peace in Myanmar?" (See Chapters 1~3.) A spiritual reading was conducted on the spot to investigate the UFOs.

RYUHO OKAWA

In the west?

A

I can see luminous flying objects faintly captured diagonally upward on the screen.

RYUHO OKAWA

Yes, there are. I can see lots of them today. We can see many stars today, maybe too many, so something different might have come, and a lot of it.

A

Huh? Wow. Look at that.

RYUHO OKAWA

What?

A

Look here... It's these. There are two on the upper left.

RYUHO OKAWA

More objects again?

A

They are blinking.

RYUHO OKAWA

There are some on the upper right. We have on the upper right.

A

I found the third one. Around here. Wow...

RYUHO OKAWA

There are also some on the upper right. So, I think we have some smaller vessels there. There are smaller ones.

A

OK. I see.

RYUHO OKAWA

The object that is mainly captured on the camera looks close to orange to the naked eye. It is blinking quite a lot and moving. I feel there are living beings in it. I also sense there are quite a lot of other UFOs with living beings, but I am most curious about this one, so I want to try to communicate with it.

Earlier, when I talked to the alien in the UFO, it said it has a connection to Ms. Aung San Suu Kyi of Myanmar, so we are now trying to capture it on camera. I have been thinking it would be good to record the spiritual interview with her guardian spirit tomorrow.

Hello, the one that is captured on our camera, if you have a message to deliver, please tell us. Where are you from?

Wilmarian asks Japan to help Myanmar

RYUHO OKAWA
They are saying "Planet Wilmar." It really sounds like "Burma." Planet Wilmar. They are moving. They are saying "Planet Wilmar." So, what brings you here? They are saying they came here to ask for help.

A
Oh.

ALIEN
We are seeking for Japan's help. We want Japan to help Burma. What Japan says has quite an influence. The Western countries don't have enough understanding of Burma.

A

They are a bit far from Burma.

ALIEN

Burma's relationship with the U.K. is neither good nor bad, so we would like Japan to take more initiative.

RYUHO OKAWA

It is a Wilmarian.

A

Wilmarian.

RYUHO OKAWA

Yes. It is saying it is a Wilmarian and it has connections to Aung San Suu Kyi.

There are 13 people in the UFO, including herself, who is a long-haired brunette

A

Are you a female?

ALIEN

Yes. I am a female with long hair.

A

Do you look like a human?

ALIEN

Yes. I am wearing an outfit.

A

Are you?

ALIEN

Yes, I am.

A

Are you black-haired?

ALIEN

Black hair... No, not black hair. I am a brunette.

A

How many people does your UFO hold?

ALIEN

There are 13 people on board now.

A

Are there male and female?

ALIEN

Yes. There are three males on board. They are mainly pilots and security guards. But the main crew are female.

The leaders of Myanmar are Buddhists, so they cry out for Buddha's help

A

So, space people who have a spiritual connection to the people living in Myanmar came.

ALIEN

Yes. We, from space, are concerned about the situation. We understand things are tough with China, but things will also be bad for Myanmar if the situation is left as it is, so we would like Happy Science to get involved.

There are only eight Happy Science followers in Myanmar, but monks are being killed and Aung San Suu Kyi is being put under house arrest. I do not think the problem can be solved without help from foreign countries.

A
From the perspective of space, how do you see the current situation in Myanmar?

ALIEN
Hopeless. Almost hopeless. Ms. Suu Kyi is an old woman at the age of 75 and actually does not have much strength left to lead the country. There are no powerful people to succeed her, nor anyone strong enough to confront the military.

Other leaders of the country are monks, like those who were massacred last time. This means the leaders of the country are Buddhists. So, they are all calling out for Buddha. They are asking for Buddha's help, so Buddha's... we ask Buddha to save them, or give them mercy.

2

China is Conspiring to Take Over Myanmar

China is trying to take control of Myanmar's military

A

I think there are value conflicts going on in Myanmar.

ALIEN

Yes. Suu Kyi studied abroad, and she wants to make Myanmar a democratic country and a country like Japan. But the Myanmar military thinks, "The cultural level of our people is low, so we have to make them obey by force. It is much too early to shift to democracy because the people have not reached that level. We cannot take off yet."

The military's basic idea is that Myanmar cannot build a society yet unless they force the people into labor and submission. It is a military-first policy.

A

Now in Hong Kong, there are anti-China movements going on, and something similar is happening in Thailand.

ALIEN

Something like that is also happening in Thailand.

A

We recently published the book titled, *The Xi Jinping Thought Now*. (See p. 192.)

ALIEN

Yes.

A

In this book, it says aliens from the dark side are reaching out to countries that aim, like China, to establish a totalitarian system.

ALIEN

China says it has successfully brought together 1.4 billion people, made great development, and formed a powerful military, so there is nothing more to be said. It does not want a political system like that of the U.S. under which people are always fighting. In contrast, China says its form of government is complete and is spreading such political thought.

It says the Western countries have been doing bad things, disturbing the countries united with harmony and order. This is how China is encouraging those who are attempting to rule the country by military force.

A

Do you think a similar power from outer space is working on the current junta of Myanmar?

ALIEN

From outer space? Rather, it's China that is already reaching out.

A

Oh, you mean through China?

ALIEN

Right. Even if they are isolated from the U.K. or U.S., as long as they have China's assistance...

A

They will be able to survive?

ALIEN

They think they will be able to survive. Myanmar's military has already received back-channel support.

Why did the military place Ms. Suu Kyi under house arrest?

A

Myanmar denies it superficially, but you suspect China has interfered in Myanmar's political turmoil.

ALIEN

Yes. The Rohingya problem has become a weak point. The Rohingya are Muslims. They are Muslim refugees. After being expelled to Bangladesh, they returned to Myanmar. Aung San Suu Kyi did not know how to deal with this problem. Then, she needed the strong power of the military, so she compromised with the military, or appeased them, to get their support. And this weak point was attacked.

Suu Kyi's political party won a landslide victory in last year's election, but the military claimed there was a fraud in the election and launched the coup, placing Suu Kyi under house arrest. The Rohingya problem triggered the turmoil. They are Muslims. Buddhists focus on peace, so they do not match up well with Muslims. Muslims come with guns. So, Suu Kyi was not very welcoming regarding this Rohingya issue.

She could not make a decision after people wondered whether she should be expelling the Rohingya to other countries as refugees despite being a Nobel Peace laureate. This also invited criticism from the West, and Suu Kyi was isolated. Then...

A
She was caught off guard?

ALIEN
When she was isolated, the military staged the coup in one go and placed her under house arrest. Now, some public officials and police officers are siding with the citizens and resisting the military, but the 75-year-old Suu Kyi is the only one who can exercise a clear leadership. The

military thinks that she will die before long if she stays under house arrest.

China's clever strategy: pincer movement and economic war

A

You mean, there are no full-fledged standard-bearers of democratization other than Suu Kyi?

ALIEN

The military dictatorship rules the country by working with China. This is China's pincer tactics. China wants to control Myanmar or Burma, so that it can keep countries like Thailand, the Philippines, and Vietnam in check.

China is thinking about causing conflicts in such countries with pincer movement, so that Japanese companies will not be able to move their production base from China to Southeast Asian countries like Thailand, Burma, and Laos. They are quite clever in coming up with such strategy.

A

I see. They are quite ingenious in that regard.

ALIEN

They are really clever in their way of thinking. If the political situation in those countries becomes unstable, Japanese factories will suspend production and move out of there. China is really quick regarding such matter.

A

Incredible.

ALIEN

So, they are waging economic war at the same time.

China's aim is to take over Myanmar, so Myanmar's military will be a puppet government

A

I see. I have another question in relation to Myanmar being a Buddhist country.

According to our recent spiritual readings, although Thailand is a Buddhist country, Thai people do not believe Buddha will ever be reborn. Thai people's faith has become weaker and Thailand has become a Buddhist country only in the superficial sense. I think things are really tough there, but how about in Myanmar? Has Myanmar's Buddhism become like the Buddhism in Thailand, or do Burmese people still have real faith?

ALIEN
Myanmar's faith is basically Hinayana Buddhism, so there is nothing that people believe in as their God. Or, they don't know at all what Buddha is doing right now.

A
They don't know.

ALIEN
There is a king in Thailand, and the king rules on behalf of God. But there is no God in Burma. So, the military is trying to establish dictatorship and rule the country on behalf of God.

A

Are they trying to become God?

ALIEN

They are trying to come up with an emperor, like China. But in terms of ideological war, there is Chinese-like ideology affecting Myanmar behind the scenes.

A

Then, the current senior general is receiving instructions from China and becoming China's puppet. Is that right?

ALIEN

Yes. He is receiving instructions and support from China. The military will be China's puppet government. I think so.

China's aim is to take over Myanmar. It's to increase their de facto colonies, more than anything else. Next, China will need to conduct a pincer movement to get the upper hand regarding battles over the South China Sea and the East China Sea, and they also need to take Taiwan. This is why China must make more anti-West, anti-U.S., and anti-U.K. countries.

China wants to advance southward and take over the entire Indochinese Peninsula

A

This will be one of the last questions. We will be conducting a spiritual interview with the guardian spirit of the earthling Suu Kyi tomorrow, but if you, the "space being Suu Kyi" have some things to share that she cannot, please tell us.

ALIEN

Hmm. It is really scary. China wants to advance southward and take over the entire Indochinese Peninsula. They want to seize the Philippines and Taiwan, and also control all the seas to seize the entire oil region through the Maritime Silk Road. This is because the U.S. president changed and...

What can we do? This year will be a year of challenges. Should democracy be done away with? Would Myanmar be stronger if the military governs the country? This year will be a test.

Master Ryuho Okawa supports democracy. Although there are not always advantages to a religion in a democracy, people will be completely helpless if the military controls the country. The military should be brought under control by a person who is elected by ordinary citizens. In this sense, I think democracy is important.

So, we are supporting democracy now because we think it is obviously better that way. However, the problem is that Burmese people are losing faith in Buddha.

Where will China cause a conflict next?

ALIEN

Biden is now being tested, too. China is shaking him by creating flash points in places other than Hong Kong and Taiwan. This is in fact a conspiracy. China is taunting him. "Can you do it?" "What can you do?"

Next, China will start a conflict near the Chinese-Indian border. They will cause conflicts here and there to taunt the U.S. They are causing conflicts in the area around Syria and Iran, too. They are causing conflicts in many places and supporting them from behind the scenes, and shaking the Biden administration to see what they can do.

A

I see. You mean, China is testing the U.S.

ALIEN

Yes, they are.

3

The Wilmarian's Sorrow and Plea for Help

Asking about Planet Wilmar

A

By the way, this is a UFO reading, so allow me to ask you this.

ALIEN

Yes.

A

Is Planet Wilmar far from Earth?

ALIEN

Let's see. It is located about 200,000 light-years from Earth. Roughly.

A

I see. What kind of planet is it? Is there God?

ALIEN

Hmm. Basically, it's a planet of people with deep faith. It's a planet where women have a higher status.

A

Did many people come down on Myanmar from Wilmar?

ALIEN

No, not so many.

A

No?

ALIEN

Not many.

A

OK.

ALIEN

Not many. But a part of Suu Kyi's soul has connections to space, so we are watching her.

A

Then, was she born with a mission?

ALIEN

But it is very likely she won't be able to fulfill her mission as it is.

How do Wilmar people see El Cantare?

A

Do you know El Cantare?

ALIEN

I do. Of course, I do.

A

How do Wilmar people see El Cantare?

ALIEN

We think He is a Great One, an extended figure of Shakyamuni Buddha.

A

Do all space people know that Shakyamuni Buddha is a great one?

ALIEN

Umm. I am not sure if they know Him by "Shakyamuni Buddha," but they know El Cantare and His other names.

A

Other names?

ALIEN

He has some other names.

A

Are there any other names you know?

ALIEN

Actually, I understand Him by the name "Buddha" or "Shakyamuni Buddha."

A

You do.

ALIEN

Burma is a Buddhist country, so I understand Him by those names. Also, a soul called "Ra Mu" comes often.

A

To your planet?

ALIEN

No, to the country I am watching now. Burma.

A

Oh, really?

ALIEN

Yes.

A

King Ra Mu is watching Myanmar?

ALIEN

Yes. Ra Mu is watching Southeast Asia.

A

Is he watching from time to time?

ALIEN

He is worried a bit. It was the region Japan wanted to modernize but could not. So, he wants to somehow modernize it with the help from Japan.

Beauty and peace are the main values on Wilmar

A

This is the first of my last two questions. What values or spirituality do people consider important on Planet Wilmar?

ALIEN

Beauty and peace, indeed.

A

Beauty and peace?

ALIEN

Yes.

A

What kind of beauty are you aiming for?

ALIEN

Umm. We think that if your mind is beautiful, you will look beautiful.

A

I see. How about peace? Now, Ms. Suu Kyi herself is, you know...

ALIEN

Actually, conflicts...

A

You do not like conflicts?

ALIEN

We do not like conflicts very much, but sometimes invaders attack us, so we must build an alliance with people from other planets who can fight with force, otherwise we cannot protect ourselves.

A

I see.

The Wilmarian hopes Buddhist countries will survive and develop in Asia

A

Do you have a sense of justice or idea of justice?

ALIEN

Yes. We came from our planet to protect Burma, but unfortunately, we do not have power. (Space Being) Yaidron and others are keeping an eye on Japan. (See p. 192.)

A

Right.

ALIEN

They cannot afford to think about Burma yet.

A

Do you know Yaidron?

ALIEN

Yes, we do. But he is planning to fight a stronger enemy.

A

He is planning to fight the real boss, right?

ALIEN

Yes, yes. So, we are like a police substation. Burma is easy work. The U.K., the U.S., and Japan can do anything to help Burma. It might not be the real boss, but we do not want to see a massacre in Burma. It would be sad to see Burma's Buddhism be destroyed, right?

A

Right.

ALIEN

Burma is one of the few Buddhist countries left. There are only a few countries that worship Buddhism.

Reconciliation with Muslims is very difficult. It will be a country of danger if it is taken over by Islam. I think it's better for there to be Buddhist countries in Asia, and they should develop. Some Buddhist countries perished like Tibet. Buddhism would perish from Burma. And, Thailand would be next. If the military establishes a dictatorship, there will soon come an end to Thailand as a Buddhist country. So, we must make the next move.

The UFO is diamond-shaped,
with several security vessels guarding it

A

OK. This is the last question. What shape is your UFO?

ALIEN

Is that your last question? It's diamond-shaped.

A

Diamond-shaped?

ALIEN

Yes, diamond-shaped. How should I say? It looks like Mt. Fuji and its reflection on the surface of a lake, upper side and lower side.

A

I see.

ALIEN

Something like that.

A

Combined?

ALIEN

Yes, yes. Both the upper side and the lower side.

A

How many floors?

ALIEN

We do not have floors.

A

Oh, right, there are only 13 people on board.

ALIEN

Yes. It's a diamond-shaped UFO, and it looks like the combined image of Mt. Fuji and its reflection on the lake.

A

On the screen here, there are two small dots moving along with you.

ALIEN

Yes. They are single-manned vessels.

A

They are guarding you?

ALIEN

There are in fact several vessels on the left and in the upper right, and they are guarding us.

Her position and outfit on her mother planet

A

What is your position on Planet Wilmar?

ALIEN

Me?

A

Yes.

ALIEN

Well, on Earth, I would be like a diplomat.

A

I see. How about your outfit? I said "first of my last two questions," but it certainly was not [*laughs*].

ALIEN

I am now wearing a space costume, but I wear something like sari or a dress worn by a heavenly maid while I am on our planet.

Wilmar means "those who believe in Buddha"

A

OK. Then, is there anything else you would like to say?

ALIEN

My name is Wilmar, as you may have guessed. Sorry.

A

Ms. Wilmar from Planet Wilmar.

WILMAR

Wilmar.

A

You mean, your name would be something like that if you
were to translate it in a way earthlings can understand?

WILMAR

Yes, yes. Perhaps it might be "Burma" in the local language.
In other words, I am something like an ambassador from
Burma. We say "Wilmar," so you can call me Ms. Wilmar,
or Wilmarian.

A

Does Wilmar have some kind of meaning? Oh, does it
mean Burma?

WILMAR

Yes. It roughly means "those who believe in Buddha."

A

Really.

WILMAR

Yes.

A

The UFOs are moving a bit.

RYUHO OKAWA

Are they moving?

A

They are moving downward.

RYUHO OKAWA

They are.

A

It has become difficult to capture them on the camera. Sorry.

Keep in mind that China is involved in Myanmar's military

WILMAR

OK. I hope your spiritual interview tomorrow will work out.

Regarding the military, really, we need the power of the people, the news agencies of other countries, and economic sanctions to change... We would like to get the military to accept the election results and bring democracy to the country. I want people to know that China is involved in Myanmar's military.

A

OK. I understand.

WILMAR

I'm not sure how much more time Suu Kyi has.

A

The color of the UFO (on the screen) has faded.

RYUHO OKAWA

It may disappear soon.

A

It is difficult to see you on the screen... I got your message.

WILMAR

Then, I hope Japanese people keep in mind what I said.

A

Thank you.

WILMAR

At any rate, I am happy to learn that there are Happy Science believers in Burma.

A

Yes. I understand.

RYUHO OKAWA

OK.

Afterword

Let me also say this to those who believe in what is called Hinayana Buddhism, a Buddhist sect that focuses on individual spiritual training.

Buddhism taught by Shakyamuni Buddha, with the Three Seals of Dharma—"impermanence of all things," "egolessness of all phenomena," and "perfect tranquility of nirvana"—was neither materialism nor atheism, much less a denial of the world after death.

Some "psychics" may ignore the Spirit World and spirits, but there is no true "religious leader" who ignores them.

For what purpose do people undergo religious training? For what purpose do they hold funerals and memorial services? Do you really think that seeking enlightenment means just realizing that human body is eventually reduced to ashes?

People are born with a physical body in this world to refine their minds. The very mind is your true self that lives in the Real World or the other world.

How much can you live rightly, nobly, and a life filled with love determines where you go after death. You must not be indifferent to other people's misery.

Ryuho Okawa
Master & CEO of Happy Science Group
Mar. 19, 2021

ABOUT THE AUTHOR

RYUHO OKAWA was born on July 7th 1956, in Tokushima, Japan. After graduating from the University of Tokyo with a law degree, he joined a Tokyo-based trading house. While working at its New York headquarters, he studied international finance at the Graduate Center of the City University of New York. In 1981, he attained Great Enlightenment and became aware that he is El Cantare with a mission to bring salvation to all humankind. In 1986, he established Happy Science. It now has members in over 160 countries across the world, with more than 700 local branches and temples as well as 10,000 missionary houses around the world. The total number of lectures has exceeded 3,300 (of which more than 150 are in English) and over 2,850 books (of which more than 600 are Spiritual Interview Series) have been published, many of which are translated into 37 languages. Many of the books, including *The Laws of the Sun* have become best sellers or million sellers. To date, Happy Science has produced 23 movies. The original story and original concept were given by the Executive Producer Ryuho Okawa. Recent movie titles are *Beautiful Lure–A Modern Tale of "Painted Skin"* (live-action, May 2021), *Into the Dreams… and Horror Experiences* (live-action movie scheduled to be released in August 2021), and *The Laws of the Universe–The Age of Elohim* (animation movie scheduled to be released in Fall of 2021). He has also composed the lyrics and music of over 450 songs, such as theme songs and featured songs of movies. Moreover, he is the Founder of Happy Science University and Happy Science Academy (Junior and Senior High School), Founder and President of the Happiness Realization Party, Founder and Honorary Headmaster of Happy Science Institute of Government and Management, Founder of IRH Press Co., Ltd., and the Chairperson of NEW STAR PRODUCTION Co., Ltd. and ARI Production Co., Ltd.

WHAT IS EL CANTARE?

El Cantare means "the Light of the Earth," and is the Supreme God of the Earth who has been guiding humankind since the beginning of Genesis. He is whom Jesus called Father and Muhammad called Allah, and is the Creator in Shintoism, *Ame-no-Mioya-Gami*. Different parts of El Cantare's core consciousness have descended to Earth in the past, once as Alpha and another as Elohim. His branch spirits, such as Shakyamuni Buddha and Hermes, have descended to Earth many times and helped to flourish many civilizations. To unite various religions and to integrate various fields of study in order to build a new civilization on Earth, a part of the core consciousness has descended to Earth as Master Ryuho Okawa.

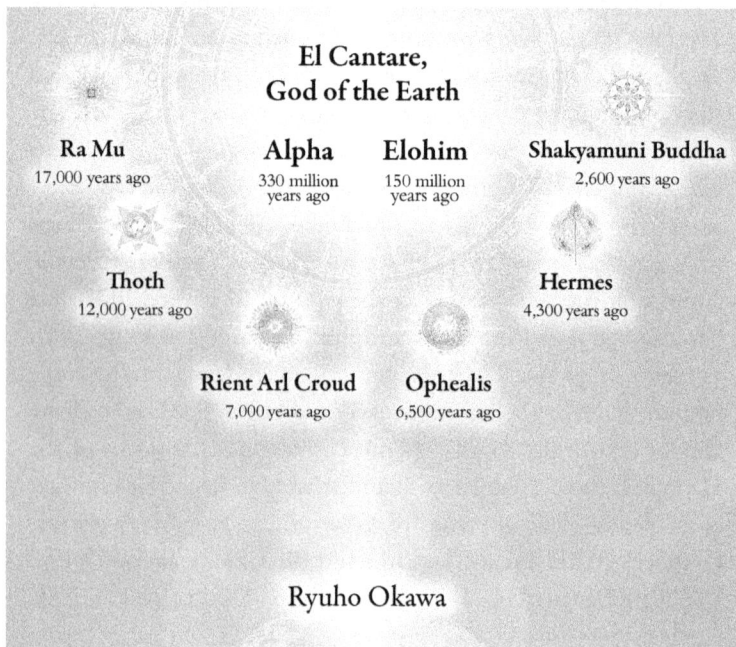

El Cantare,
God of the Earth

Ra Mu	Alpha	Elohim	Shakyamuni Buddha
17,000 years ago	330 million years ago	150 million years ago	2,600 years ago

Thoth			Hermes
12,000 years ago			4,300 years ago

Rient Arl Croud	Ophealis
7,000 years ago	6,500 years ago

Ryuho Okawa

Alpha is a part of the core consciousness of El Cantare who descended to Earth around 330 million years ago. Alpha preached Earth's Truths to harmonize and unify Earth-born humans and space people who came from other planets.

Elohim is a part of El Cantare's core consciousness who descended to Earth around 150 million years ago. He gave wisdom, mainly on the differences of light and darkness, good and evil.

Shakyamuni Buddha was born as a prince into the Shakya Clan in India around 2,600 years ago. When he was 29 years old, he renounced the world and sought enlightenment. He later attained Great Enlightenment and founded Buddhism.

Hermes is one of the 12 Olympian gods in Greek mythology, but the spiritual Truth is that he taught the teachings of love and progress around 4,300 years ago that became the origin of the current Western civilization. He is a hero that truly existed.

Ophealis was born in Greece around 6,500 years ago and was the leader who took an expedition to as far as Egypt. He is the God of miracles, prosperity, and arts, and is known as Osiris in the Egyptian mythology.

Rient Arl Croud was born as a king of the ancient Incan Empire around 7,000 years ago and taught about the mysteries of the mind. In the heavenly world, he is responsible for the interactions that take place between various planets.

Thoth was an almighty leader who built the golden age of the Atlantic civilization around 12,000 years ago. In the Egyptian mythology, he is known as god Thoth.

Ra Mu was a leader who built the golden age of the civilization of Mu around 17,000 years ago. As a religious leader and a politician, he ruled by uniting religion and politics.

WHAT IS A SPIRITUAL MESSAGE?

We are all spiritual beings living on this earth. The following is the mechanism behind Master Ryuho Okawa's spiritual messages.

1 You are a spirit

People are born into this world to gain wisdom through various experiences and return to the other world when their lives end. We are all spirits and repeat this cycle in order to refine our souls.

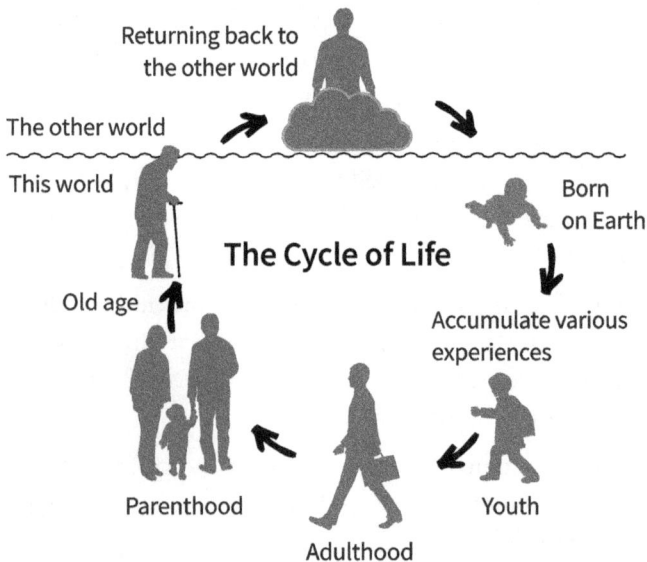

Returning back to
the other world

The other world

This world

Born
on Earth

The Cycle of Life

Old age

Accumulate various
experiences

Parenthood

Youth

Adulthood

2 You have a guardian spirit

Guardian spirits are those who protect the people who are living on this earth. Each of us has a guardian spirit that watches over us and guides us from the other world. They were us in our past life, and are identical in how we think.

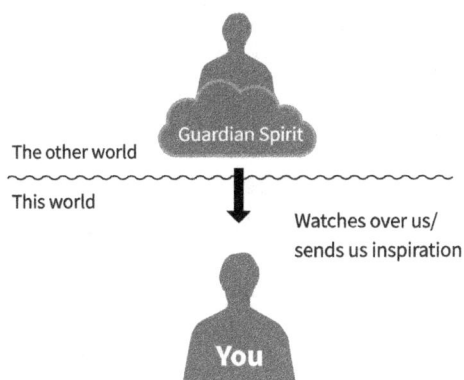

3 How spiritual messages work

Master Ryuho Okawa, through his enlightenment, is capable of summoning any spirit from anywhere in the world, including the spirit world.

Master Okawa's way of receiving spiritual messages is fundamentally different from that of other psychic mediums who undergo trances and are thereby completely taken over by the spirits they are channeling.

Master Okawa's attainment of a high level of enlightenment enables him to retain full control of his consciousness and body throughout the duration of the spiritual message. To allow the spirits to express their own thoughts and personalities freely, however, Master Okawa usually softens the dominancy of his consciousness. This way, he is able to keep his own philosophies out of the way and ensure that the spiritual messages are pure expressions of the spirits he is channeling.

Since guardian spirits think at the same subconscious level as the person living on earth, Master Okawa can summon the spirit and find out what the person on earth is actually thinking. If the person has already returned to the other world, the spirit can give messages to the people living on earth through Master Okawa.

Since 2009, more than 1,200 sessions of spiritual messages have been openly recorded by Master Okawa, and the majority of these have been published. Spiritual messages from the guardian spirits of people living today such as Donald Trump, former Japanese Prime Minister Shinzo Abe and Chinese President Xi Jinping, as well as spiritual messages sent from the spirit world by Jesus Christ, Muhammad, Thomas Edison, Mother Teresa, Steve Jobs and Nelson Mandela are just a tiny pack of spiritual messages that were published so far.

Domestically, in Japan, these spiritual messages are being read by a wide range of politicians and mass media, and the high-level contents of these books are delivering an impact even more on politics, news and public opinion. In recent years, there have been spiritual messages recorded in English, and English translations are being done on the spiritual messages given in Japanese. These have been published overseas, one after another, and have started to shake the world.

1 The guardian spirit / spirit in the other world...

2 Goes inside Master Okawa in this world

3 Master Okawa speaks the words of the guardian spirit / spirit

For more about spiritual messages and a complete list of books in the Spiritual Interview Series, visit **okawabooks.com**

ABOUT HAPPY SCIENCE

Happy Science is a global movement that empowers individuals to find purpose and spiritual happiness and to share that happiness with their families, societies, and the world. With more than 12 million members around the world, Happy Science aims to increase awareness of spiritual truths and expand our capacity for love, compassion, and joy so that together we can create the kind of world we all wish to live in.

Activities at Happy Science are based on the Principles of Happiness (Love, Wisdom, Self-Reflection, and Progress). These principles embrace worldwide philosophies and beliefs, transcending boundaries of culture and religions.

Love teaches us to give ourselves freely without expecting anything in return; it encompasses giving, nurturing, and forgiving.

Wisdom leads us to the insights of spiritual truths, and opens us to the true meaning of life and the will of God (the universe, the highest power, Buddha).

Self-Reflection brings a mindful, nonjudgmental lens to our thoughts and actions to help us find our truest selves—the essence of our souls—and deepen our connection to the highest power. It helps us attain a clean and peaceful mind and leads us to the right life path.

Progress emphasizes the positive, dynamic aspects of our spiritual growth—actions we can take to manifest and spread happiness around the world. It's a path that not only expands our soul growth, but also furthers the collective potential of the world we live in.

PROGRAMS AND EVENTS

The doors of Happy Science are open to all. We offer a variety of programs and events, including self-exploration and self-growth programs, spiritual seminars, meditation and contemplation sessions, study groups, and book events.

Our programs are designed to:
* Deepen your understanding of your purpose and meaning in life
* Improve your relationships and increase your capacity to love unconditionally
* Attain peace of mind, decrease anxiety and stress, and feel positive
* Gain deeper insights and a broader perspective on the world
* Learn how to overcome life's challenges
   ... and much more.

*For more information, visit **happy-science.org**.*

OUR ACTIVITIES

Happy Science does other various activities to provide support for those in need.

◆ **You Are An Angel! General Incorporated Association**

Happy Science has a volunteer network in Japan that encourages and supports children with disabilities as well as their parents and guardians.

◆ **Never Mind School for Truancy**

At 'Never Mind,' we support students who find it very challenging to attend schools in Japan. We also nurture their self-help spirit and power to rebound against obstacles in life based on Master Okawa's teachings and faith.

◆ **"Prevention Against Suicide" Campaign since 2003**

A nationwide campaign to reduce suicides; over 20,000 people commit suicide every year in Japan. "The Suicide Prevention Website-Words of Truth for You-" presents spiritual prescriptions for worries such as depression, lost love, extramarital affairs, bullying and work-related problems, thereby saving many lives.

◆ **Support for Anti-bullying Campaigns**

Happy Science provides support for a group of parents and guardians, Network to Protect Children from Bullying, a general incorporated foundation launched in Japan to end bullying, including those that can even be called a criminal offense. So far, the network received more than 5,000 cases and resolved 90% of them.

- **The Golden Age Scholarship**

  This scholarship is granted to students who can contribute greatly and bring a hopeful future to the world.

- **Success No.1**
  Buddha's Truth Afterschool Academy

  Happy Science has over 180 classrooms throughout Japan and in several cities around the world that focus on afterschool education for children. The education focuses on faith and morals in addition to supporting children's school studies.

- **Angel Plan V**

  For children under the age of kindergarten, Happy Science holds classes for nurturing healthy, positive, and creative boys and girls.

- **Future Stars Training Department**

  The Future Stars Training Department was founded within the Happy Science Media Division with the goal of nurturing talented individuals to become successful in the performing arts and entertainment industry.

- **NEW STAR PRODUCTION Co., Ltd.**
  ARI Production Co., Ltd.

  We have companies to nurture actors and actresses, artists, and vocalists. They are also involved in film production.

ABOUT HAPPINESS REALIZATION PARTY

The Happiness Realization Party (HRP) was founded in May 2009 by Master Ryuho Okawa as part of the Happy Science Group to offer concrete and proactive solutions to the current issues such as military threats from North Korea and China and the long-term economic recession. HRP aims to implement drastic reforms of the Japanese government, thereby bringing peace and prosperity to Japan. To accomplish this, HRP proposes two key policies:

1) Strengthening the national security and the Japan-U.S. alliance, which plays a vital role in the stability of Asia.

2) Improving the Japanese economy by implementing drastic tax cuts, taking monetary easing measures and creating new major industries.

HRP advocates that Japan should offer a model of a religious nation that allows diverse values and beliefs to coexist, and that contributes to global peace.

*For more information, visit **en.hr-party.jp***

HAPPY SCIENCE ACADEMY
JUNIOR AND SENIOR HIGH SCHOOL

Happy Science Academy Junior and Senior High School is a boarding school founded with the goal of educating the future leaders of the world who can have a big vision, persevere, and take on new challenges.

Currently, there are two campuses in Japan; the Nasu Main Campus in Tochigi Prefecture, founded in 2010, and the Kansai Campus in Shiga Prefecture, founded in 2013.

Nasu Main Campus

Kansai Campus

CONTACT INFORMATION

Happy Science is a worldwide organization with faith centers around the globe. For a comprehensive list of centers, visit the worldwide directory at *happy-science.org*. The following are some of the many Happy Science locations:

UNITED STATES AND CANADA

New York
79 Franklin St., New York, NY 10013
Phone: 212-343-7972
Fax: 212-343-7973
Email: ny@happy-science.org
Website: happyscience-usa.org

New Jersey
725 River Rd, #102B, Edgewater, NJ 07020
Phone: 201-313-0127
Fax: 201-313-0120
Email: nj@happy-science.org
Website: happyscience-usa.org

Florida
5208 8th St., Zephyrhills, FL 33542
Phone: 813-715-0000
Fax: 813-715-0010
Email: florida@happy-science.org
Website: happyscience-usa.org

Atlanta
1874 Piedmont Ave., NE Suite 360-C
Atlanta, GA 30324
Phone: 404-892-7770
Email: atlanta@happy-science.org
Website: happyscience-usa.org

San Francisco
525 Clinton St.
Redwood City, CA 94062
Phone & Fax: 650-363-2777
Email: sf@happy-science.org
Website: happyscience-usa.org

Los Angeles
1590 E. Del Mar Blvd., Pasadena, CA 91106
Phone: 626-395-7775
Fax: 626-395-7776
Email: la@happy-science.org
Website: happyscience-usa.org

Orange County
10231 Slater Ave., #204
Fountain Valley, CA 92708
Phone: 714-659-1501
Email: oc@happy-science.org
Website: happyscience-usa.org

San Diego
7841 Balboa Ave., Suite #202
San Diego, CA 92111
Phone: 626-395-7775
Fax: 626-395-7776
E-mail: sandiego@happy-science.org
Website: happyscience-usa.org

Hawaii
Phone: 808-591-9772
Fax: 808-591-9776
Email: hi@happy-science.org
Website: happyscience-usa.org

Kauai
3343 Kanakolu Street, Suite 5
Lihue, HI 96766, U.S.A.
Phone: 808-822-7007
Fax: 808-822-6007
Email: kauai-hi@happy-science.org
Website: happyscience-usa.org

Toronto

845 The Queensway
Etobicoke ON M8Z 1N6 Canada
Phone: 1-416-901-3747
Email: toronto@happy-science.org
Website: happy-science.ca

Vancouver

#201-2607 East 49th Avenue
Vancouver, BC, V5S 1J9, Canada
Phone: 1-604-437-7735
Fax: 1-604-437-7764
Email: vancouver@happy-science.org
Website: happy-science.ca

INTERNATIONAL

Tokyo

1-6-7 Togoshi, Shinagawa
Tokyo, 142-0041 Japan
Phone: 81-3-6384-5770
Fax: 81-3-6384-5776
Email: tokyo@happy-science.org
Website: happy-science.org

Seoul

74, Sadang-ro 27-gil,
Dongjak-gu, Seoul, Korea
Phone: 82-2-3478-8777
Fax: 82-2-3478-9777
Email: korea@happy-science.org
Website: happyscience-korea.org

London

3 Margaret St.
London,W1W 8RE United Kingdom
Phone: 44-20-7323-9255
Fax: 44-20-7323-9344
Email: eu@happy-science.org
Website: happyscience-uk.org

Taipei

No. 89, Lane 155, Dunhua N. Road
Songshan District, Taipei City 105, Taiwan
Phone: 886-2-2719-9377
Fax: 886-2-2719-5570
Email: taiwan@happy-science.org
Website: happyscience-tw.org

Sydney

516 Pacific Hwy, Lane Cove North,
NSW 2066, Australia
Phone: 61-2-9411-2877
Fax: 61-2-9411-2822
Email: sydney@happy-science.org

Malaysia

No 22A, Block 2, Jalil Link Jalan Jalil Jaya 2,
Bukit Jalil 57000, Kuala Lumpur, Malaysia
Phone: 60-3-8998-7877
Fax: 60-3-8998-7977
Email: malaysia@happy-science.org
Website: happyscience.org.my

Brazil Headquarters

Rua. Domingos de Morais 1154,
Vila Mariana, Sao Paulo SP
CEP 04010-100, Brazil
Phone: 55-11-5088-3800
Email: sp@happy-science.org
Website: happyscience.com.br

Nepal

Kathmandu Metropolitan City Ward
No. 15,
Ring Road, Kimdol,
Sitapaila Kathmandu, Nepal
Phone: 97-714-272931
Email: nepal@happy-science.org

Jundiai

Rua Congo, 447, Jd. Bonfiglioli
Jundiai-CEP, 13207-340
Phone: 55-11-4587-5952
Email: jundiai@happy-science.org

Uganda

Plot 877 Rubaga Road, Kampala
P.O. Box 34130, Kampala, Uganda
Phone: 256-79-4682-121
Email: uganda@happy-science.org
Website: happyscience-uganda.org

ABOUT IRH PRESS

IRH Press Co., Ltd., based in Tokyo, was founded in 1987 as a publishing division of Happy Science. IRH Press publishes religious and spiritual books, journals, magazines and also operates broadcast and film production enterprises. For more information, visit *okawabooks.com.*

Follow us on:

Facebook: Okawa Books   **Twitter:** Okawa Books
Goodreads: Ryuho Okawa   **Instagram:** OkawaBooks
Pinterest: Okawa Books

———— NEWSLETTER ————

To receive book related news, promotions and events, please subscribe to our newsletter below.

https://okawabooks.us11.list-manage.com/subscribe?u=1fc70960eefd92668052ab7f8
&id=2fbd8150ef

———— MEDIA ————

OKAWA BOOK CLUB

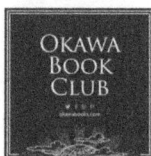

A conversation about Ryuho Okawa's titles, topics ranging from self-help, current affairs, spirituality and religions.

Available at iTunes, Spotify and Amazon Music.

Apple iTunes:
https://podcasts.apple.com/us/podcast/okawa-book-club/id1527893043

Spotify:
https://open.spotify.com/show/09mpgX2iJ6stVm4eBRdo2b

Amazon Music:
https://music.amazon.com/podcasts/7b759f24-ff72-4523-bfee-24f48294998f/Okawa-Book-Club

BOOKS BY RYUHO OKAWA

RYUHO OKAWA'S LAWS SERIES

The Laws Series is an annual volume of books that are mainly comprised of Ryuho Okawa's lectures on various topics that highlight principles and guidelines for the activities of Happy Science every year. *The Laws of the Sun*, the first publication of the laws series, ranked in the annual best-selling list in Japan in 1987. Since then, all of the laws series' titles have ranked in the annual best-selling list for more than two decades, setting socio-cultural trends in Japan and around the world.

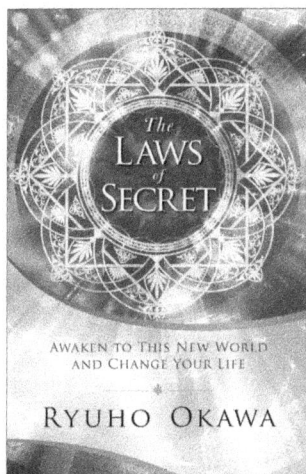

The 27th Laws Series

THE LAWS OF SECRET

AWAKEN TO THIS NEW WORLD
AND CHANGE YOUR LIFE

Paperback • 248 pages • $16.95
ISBN: 978-1-942125-81-5

Our physical world coexists with the multi-dimensional spirit world and we are constantly interacting with some kind of spiritual energy, whether positive or negative, without consciously realizing it. This book reveals how our lives are affected by invisible influences, including the spiritual reasons behind influenza, the novel coronavirus infection, and other illnesses.

The new view of the world in this book will inspire you to change your life in a better direction, and to become someone who can give hope and courage to others in this age of confusion.

*For a complete list of books, visit **okawabooks.com***

THE TRILOGY

The first three volumes of the Laws Series, *The Laws of the Sun*, *The Golden Laws*, and *The Nine Dimensions* make a trilogy that completes the basic framework of the teachings of God's Truths. *The Laws of the Sun* discusses the structure of God's Laws, *The Golden Laws* expounds on the doctrine of time, and *The Nine Dimensions* reveals the nature of space.

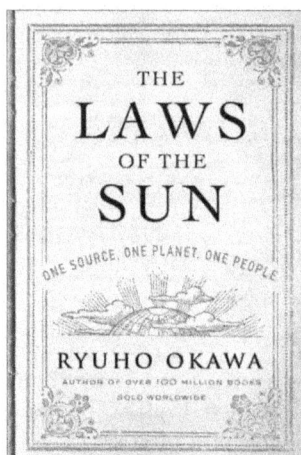

THE LAWS OF THE SUN

ONE SOURCE, ONE PLANET, ONE PEOPLE

Paperback • 288 pages • $15.95
ISBN: 978-1-942125-43-3

IMAGINE IF YOU COULD ASK GOD why He created this world and what spiritual laws He used to shape us—and everything around us. If we could understand His designs and intentions, we could discover what our goals in life should be and whether our actions move us closer to those goals or farther away.

At a young age, a spiritual calling prompted Ryuho Okawa to outline what he innately understood to be universal truths for all humankind. In *The Laws of the Sun*, Okawa outlines these laws of the universe and provides a road map for living one's life with greater purpose and meaning.

In this powerful book, Ryuho Okawa reveals the transcendent nature of consciousness and the secrets of our multidimensional universe and our place in it. By understanding the different stages of love and following the Buddhist Eightfold Path, he believes we can speed up our eternal process of development. *The Laws of the Sun* shows the way to realize true happiness—a happiness that continues from this world through the other.

*For a complete list of books, visit **okawabooks.com***

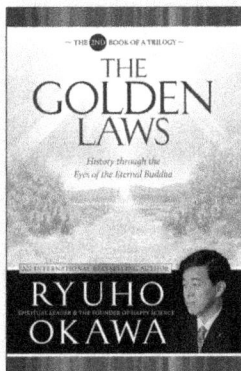

THE GOLDEN LAWS
HISTORY THROUGH THE EYES OF THE ETERNAL BUDDHA

Paperback • 201 pages • $14.95
ISBN: 978-1-941779-81-1

Throughout history, Great Guiding Spirits of Light have been present on Earth in both the East and the West at crucial points in human history to further our spiritual development. *The Golden Laws* reveals how Divine Plan has been unfolding on Earth, and outlines 5,000 years of the secret history of humankind. Once we understand the true course of history, through past, present and into the future, we cannot help but become aware of the significance of our spiritual mission in the present age.

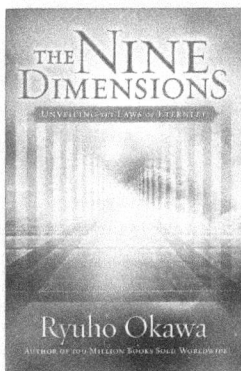

THE NINE DIMENSIONS
UNVEILING THE LAWS OF ETERNITY

Paperback • 168 pages • $15.95
ISBN: 978-0-982698-56-3

This book is a window into the mind of our loving God, who designed this world and the vast, wondrous world of our afterlife as a school with many levels through which our souls learn and grow. When the religions and cultures of the world discover the truth of their common spiritual origin, they will be inspired to accept their differences, come together under faith in God, and build an era of harmony and peaceful progress on Earth.

---

*For a complete list of books, visit **okawabooks.com***

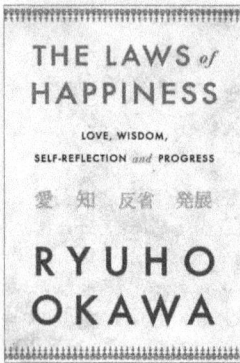

THE LAWS OF HAPPINESS
LOVE, WISDOM, SELF-REFLECTION AND PROGRESS

Paperback • 264 pages • $16.95
ISBN: 978-1-942125-70-9

This book endeavors to answer the question, "What is true happiness?" This milestone text introduces four distinct principles, based on the "Laws of Mind" and sourced from Okawa's real-world experience, to guide readers towards sustainable happiness. Okawa's four "Principles of Happiness" present an easy, yet profound framework to ground this rapidly advanced and highly competitive society. In practice, Okawa outlines pragmatic steps to revitalize our ambition to lead a happier and meaningful life.

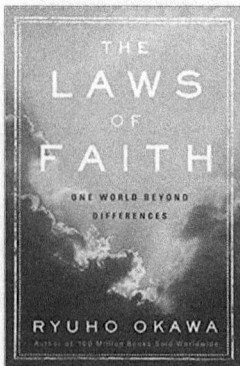

THE LAWS OF FAITH
ONE WORLD BEYOND DIFFERENCES

Paperback • 208 pages • $15.95
ISBN: 978-1-942125-34-1

Ryuho Okawa preaches at the core of a new universal religion from various angles while integrating logical and spiritual viewpoints in mind with current world situations. This book offers us the key to accept diversities beyond differences in ethnicity, religion, race, gender, descent, and so on, harmonize the individuals and nations and create a world filled with peace and prosperity.

*For a complete list of books, visit **okawabooks.com***

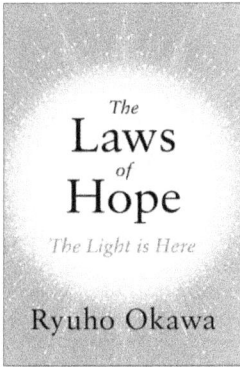

THE LAWS OF HOPE
THE LIGHT IS HERE

Paperback • 224 pages • $16.95
ISBN:978-1-942125-76-1

This book provides ways to bring light and hope to ourselves through our own efforts, even in the midst of sufferings and adversities. Inspired by a wish to bring happiness, success, and hope to humanity, Okawa shows us how to look at and think about our lives and circumstances. He says that hopes come true when we have the right mindset inside us.

THE LAWS OF JUSTICE
HOW WE CAN SOLVE WORLD CONFLICTS AND BRING PEACE

Paperback • 208 pages • $15.95
ISBN: 978-1-942125-05-1

This book shows what global justice is from a comprehensive perspective of the Supreme God. Becoming aware of this view will let us embrace differences in beliefs, recognize other people's divine nature, and love and forgive one another. It will also become the key to solving the issues we face, whether they're religious, political, societal, economic, or academic, and help the world become a better and safer world for all of us living today.

*For a complete list of books, visit **okawabooks.com***

EXPLORING THE TRUE TEACHING OF BUDDHA

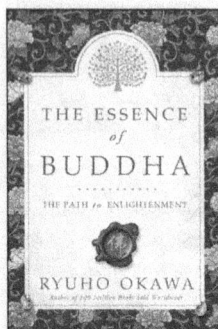

THE ESSENCE OF BUDDHA
THE PATH TO ENLIGHTENMENT

Paperback • 208 pages • $14.95
ISBN: 978-1-942125-06-8

In this book, Ryuho Okawa imparts in simple and accessible language his wisdom about the essence of Shakyamuni Buddha's philosophy of life and enlightenment—teachings that have been inspiring people all over the world for over 2,500 years. By offering a new perspective on core Buddhist thoughts, Okawa brings these teachings to life for modern people. This book distills a way of life that anyone can practice to achieve a life of self-growth, compassionate living, and true happiness.

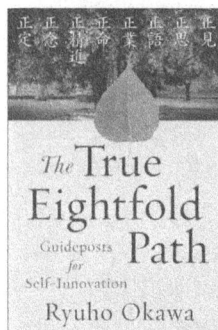

THE TRUE EIGHTFOLD PATH
GUIDEPOSTS FOR SELF-INNOVATION

Paperback • 272 pages • $16.95
ISBN: 978-1-942125-80-8

This book explains how we can apply the Eightfold Path, one of the main pillars of Shakyamuni Buddha's teachings, as everyday guideposts in the modern-age to achieve self-innovation to live better and make positive changes in these uncertain times.

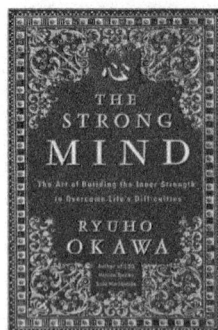

THE STRONG MIND
THE ART OF BUILDING THE INNER STRENGTH TO OVERCOME LIFE'S DIFFICULTIES

Paperback • 192 pages • $15.95
ISBN: 978-1-942125-36-5

The strong mind is what we need to rise time and again, and to move forward no matter what difficulties we face in life. This book will inspire and empower you to take courage, develop a mature and cultivated heart, and achieve resilience and hardiness so that you can break through the barriers of your limits and keep winning in the battle of your life.

*For a complete list of books, visit **okawabooks.com***

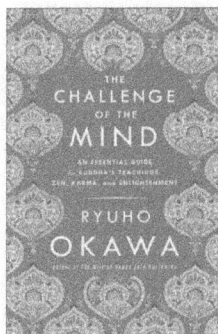

THE CHALLENGE OF THE MIND
AN ESSENTIAL GUIDE TO BUDDHA'S TEACHINGS: ZEN, KARMA AND ENLIGHTENMENT

Paperback • 208 pages • $16.95
ISBN: 978-1-942125-45-7

In this book, Ryuho Okawa explains essential Buddhist tenets and how to put them into practice. Enlightenment is not just an abstract idea but one that everyone can experience to some extent. Okawa offers a solid basis of reason and intellectual understanding to Buddhist concepts. By applying these basic principles to our lives, we can direct our minds to higher ideals and create a bright future for ourselves and others.

THE LAWS OF GREAT ENLIGHTENMENT
ALWAYS WALK WITH BUDDHA

Paperback • 232 pages • $17.95
ISBN: 978-1-942125-62-4

Constant self-blame for mistakes, setbacks, or failures and feelings of unforgivingness toward others are hard to overcome. Through the power of enlightenment we can learn to forgive ourselves and others, overcome life's problems, and courageously create a brighter future ourselves. The Laws of Great Enlightenment addresses the core problems of life that people often struggle with and offers advice on how to overcome them based on spiritual truths.

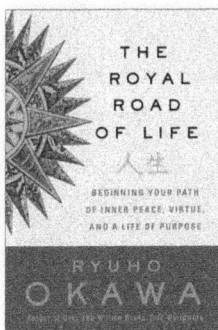

THE ROYAL ROAD OF LIFE
BEGINNING YOUR PATH OF INNER PEACE, VIRTUE, AND A LIFE OF PURPOSE

Paperback • 224 pages • $16.95
ISBN: 978-1-942125-53-2

With over 30 years of lectures and teachings spanning diverse topics of faith, self-growth, leadership (and more), Ryuho Okawa presents the profound eastern wisdom that he has cultivated on his approach to life. The Royal Road of Life illuminates a path to becoming a person of virtue, whose character and depth will move and inspire others towards the same meaningful destination.

*For a complete list of books, visit **okawabooks.com***

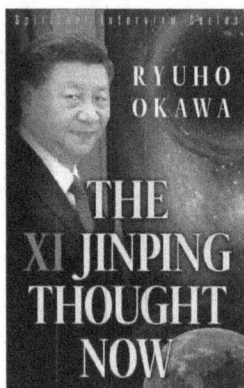

THE XI JINPING THOUGHT NOW

Paperback • 212 pages • $13.95
ISBN: 978-1-943928-05-7

With the launch of Biden administration in the U.S. and the 100th anniversary of the founding of the Chinese Communist Party approaching, China has been expanding its military threat and reinforcing its influence over the world. What urges China to seek global hegemony? This book unveils the "dark being" behind the Xi Jinping Thought.

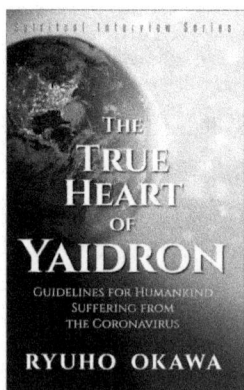

THE TRUE HEART OF YAIDRON

GUIDELINES FOR HUMANKIND SUFFERING FROM THE CORONAVIRUS

Paperback • 144 pages • $11.95
ISBN: 978-1-943928-04-0

What are the real cause and evil schemes behind the worldwide coronavirus crisis? Out of compassion, this book reveals truths about the all-out global war now being waged by the evil power in East Asia that's destroying the power of the people. Discover the movement that's trying to bring together the powers of the West, India, and Asia by the belief of "With Savior," to save humankind and create the new golden future of Earth.

---

*For a complete list of books, visit **okawabooks.com***

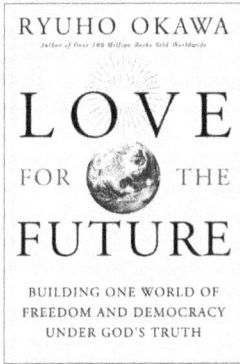

LOVE FOR THE FUTURE
BUILDING ONE WORLD OF FREEDOM AND DEMOCRACY UNDER GOD'S TRUTH

Paperback • 312 pages • $15.95
ISBN: 978-1-942125-60-0

This is a compilation of select international lectures given by Ryuho Okawa during his (ongoing) global missionary tours. While conflicting values of justice exist, this book espouses freedom and democracy are vital principles for global unification that will resolutely foster peace and shared prosperity, if adopted universally.

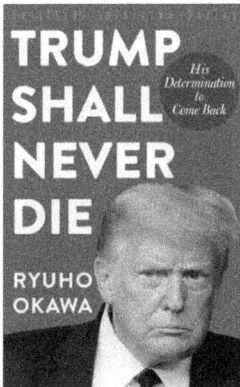

TRUMP SHALL NEVER DIE
HIS DETERMINATION TO COME BACK

Paperback • 206 pages • $11.95
ISBN: 978-1-943928-08-8

This book unveiled Mr. Donald Trump's true thoughts never reported by the media through spiritual interview with the guardian spirit of him. The topics include the "madness" found in GAFA and the mainstream media, Mr. Trump's views on the coronavirus vaccine and global warming, and the true aim of "Make America Great Again."

For a complete list of books, visit ***okawabooks.com***

*For a complete list of books, visit **okawabooks.com***

MUSIC BY RYUHO OKAWA

THE THUNDER

a composition for repelling the Coronavirus

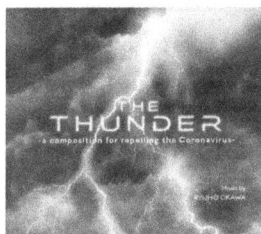

We have been granted this music from our Lord. It will repel away the novel Coronavirus originated in China. Experience this magnificent powerful music.

Search on YouTube

the thunder coronavirus 🔍 for a short ad!

THE EXORCISM

prayer music for repelling Lost Spirits

Feel the divine vibrations of this Japanese and Western exorcising symphony to banish all evil possessions you suffer from and to purify your space!

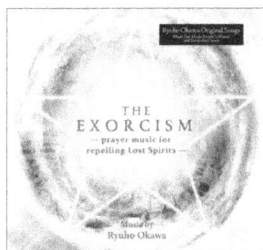

Search on YouTube

the exorcism repelling 🔍 for a short ad!

🎧 **Listen online**
Spotify iTunes Amazon

CD available at amazon.com, and Happy Science local branches & shoja (temples)

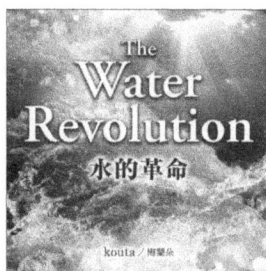

www.ingramcontent.com/pod-product-compliance
Lightning Source LLC
Chambersburg PA
CBHW032056020426
42335CB00011B/359